Sarah Geraldina Stock

The Story of Uganda and the Victoria Nyanza Mission

Sarah Geraldina Stock

The Story of Uganda and the Victoria Nyanza Mission

ISBN/EAN: 9783743351295

Manufactured in Europe, USA, Canada, Australia, Japa

Cover: Foto ©ninafisch / pixelio.de

Manufactured and distributed by brebook publishing software (www.brebook.com)

Sarah Geraldina Stock

The Story of Uganda and the Victoria Nyanza Mission

THE STORY OF UGANDA

AND THE

VICTORIA NYANZA MISSION

BY

SARAH GERALDINA STOCK

WITH FIFTEEN ILLUSTRATIONS

FLEMING H. REVELL COMPANY
NEW YORK | CHICAGO
30 Union Square, East | 148-150 Madison Street
Publishers of Evangelical Literature

48362

INTRODUCTION.

'A POSSESSION of a burying-place' was the first thing acquired by the patriarch of old in the land which was promised to him and to his heirs for ever. A woman's funeral inaugurated the beginning of Abraham's ownership in Canaan. As the mournful procession passed up the field and beneath the spreading trees of Machpelah, to the cave which was to be Sarah's last earthly resting-place, did there pass before the tear-dimmed eyes of her husband a vision of the future, when one of his children's children should be crowned as king in the neighbouring city of Hebron? Under the teaching of the Spirit of God he looked for something even higher—for a 'city which hath foundations, whose Builder and Maker is God.' Yet the purpose of God was to be fulfilled literally. And as the long years passed away, others beside Sarah were interred in the same spot, while the body of Jacob's beloved wife Rachel was laid to rest some miles further north, at Bethlehem. These graves were as a seal set upon the land of Canaan, marking it out as the inheritance of the people whom God had chosen. And although the Israelites grew into a nation, lived, died, and were buried in Egypt, the body of him under whose auspices they had settled in that country was kept, embalmed and uninterred, until the time came when it should be laid to rest in the land, no more of Canaan, but of Israel.

Pass over 3,200 years (in round numbers), and look at the funeral of another woman, the wife of a 'stranger in a strange land.' A solitary mourner, in much bodily weakness, follows the coffin up the sandy beach, and a little farther on, under the shade of the palms and mangoes, the body of Rosine Krapf is laid to rest, the waters of Mombasa inlet chanting the requiem, while the blue hills of Rabai and of Shimba looked down upon the novel sight of a Christian burial. Here is the first occupation of East Africa by a servant of Christ. On that day the land was taken possession of in the name of Him whose rightful inheritance it is. A day or two after her motherless babe was buried in the same place. But the bereaved husband and father, steeped in sorrow, yet strong in faith, wrote thus concerning the hallowed spot:—

'Tell our friends that there is on the East African coast a lonely grave of a member of the Mission cause connected with your Society. This is a sign that you have commenced the struggle with this part of the world; and as the victories of the Church are gained by stepping over the graves of many of her members, you may be the more convinced that the hour is at hand when you are summoned to the conversion of Africa from its eastern shore.'

A few years later, up among the hills of Rabai, there is another funeral. The piece of ground newly purchased of the Wanika by Krapf's fellow-labourer, Rebmann, is hallowed by the interment there of the young missionary Pffefferle, whose life has been given

for the Redeemer's cause in these regions. And once more Krapf takes his pen and writes, not in the language of despondency, but of hope and courage :—
'The first resident of the new Mission ground is a dead person of the missionary circle. Our God bids us first build a cemetery before we build a church or dwelling-house; showing us by this lesson that the resurrection of East Africa must be effected by our own destruction.'

Yet for some time longer the conquest of East Africa for Christ seems almost at a standstill. Krapf, worn out with labours and hardships, returns to Europe, and occupies himself with linguistic work. Rebmann grows old, infirm, and blind at his post, but will not leave it. Both have their eyes fixed on the goal, which to most men would have seemed a mere idle vision, the setting up of Christ's kingdom, not only on the coast, but in the interior of this vast country, knowing that His mark is on the land, in the graves of His faithful servants.

And at length the time comes for the purpose of God to be fulfilled. Close to that solitary grave on the shore a Mission settlement is planted. Round about that grave on the heights another settlement grows and flourishes. In Frere Town and in Kisulutini the Word of God is taught, and souls are won for the Saviour. A part of the land has been conquered for Christ.

Look back now once more at Israelitish history. The time at length comes for the conquest of the land of Canaan by the hosts of the Lord. The Jordan is crossed, and Jericho and Ai taken by storm. And this first foothold being gained in the land, Joshua and the

Israelites proceed to do what under ordinary circumstances would have seemed a most foolish thing, and have probably brought upon them defeat and destruction. Instead of advancing carefully, step by step, they march boldly forward into the very centre of the country, not to erect a strong fort, but to set up an altar to God, and write on the stones a copy of His law. In the lovely valley of Shechem, in the midst of that hostile and heathen country, the solemn assembly is held, and from the opposite hills the blessings for the obedient and the curses for the disobedient are pronounced. This was done in no mere bravado, but at the express command of God, given some months before. They 'made haste, and delayed not, to keep His commandments.' And they found obedience the path to victory.

We find a parallel to this in the action of the Church Missionary Society in East Africa. Having obtained a foothold on the coast, they proceeded to send a missionary expedition into the heart of the country. Instead of advancing gradually inland, they ventured at once to occupy one of the countries on the shores of the great inland sea known by the name of the Victoria Nyanza, and this one of the most fertile, wealthy, and powerful kingdoms of the whole continent. It was in 1875 that Frere Town rose up on the coast opposite Mombasa, as a refuge for liberated slaves, and a place where they might be trained and educated. And the very next year saw the little band set forth to start a Mission on the Victoria Nyanza. It was in no spirit of haste or of presumption that this step was taken, but in obedience to what appeared to the Church Missionary Society Committee as a direct call from

INTRODUCTION.

God, coming to them through the remarkable chain of events connected with the opening up of East Africa, and the bringing to light the marvellous country of Uganda. The advance was made into a strange land, a land of heathen darkness, and there the Word of God was introduced, and the law of God proclaimed. And though the powers of hell have fought against it at every step, that Word has held on its course, and has been victorious over all opposition. It is a wondrous story. And though the future of Uganda may look uncertain, and dark clouds may loom over the brightness which has risen on the land, we may and must trust Him who has done the work to watch over and uphold His own.

By the courtesy of Messrs. Sampson Low and Co., we are enabled to give the engravings of Rubaga, and Mtesa and his chiefs.

CONTENTS.

	PAGE
I. A CALL FROM AFAR	13
II. A LAND OF DARKNESS	24
III. FROM THE SHORES OF ENGLAND TO NYANZA	35
IV. THE GOAL REACHED	50
V. SOWING THE SEED AMID DIFFICULTIES	63
VI. THE SEED SPRINGING UP	76
VII. THE BEGINNING OF PERSECUTION	91
VIII. THE MARTYR BISHOP	109
IX. THE GREAT PERSECUTION	125
X. FRESH LABOURERS AND FRESH SORROWS	141
XI. THE REVOLUTION IN UGANDA	157
XII. THE CHURCH IN EXILE	172
XIII. LABOUR AND REST BY THE LAKE	186
XIV. A NEW ERA IN UGANDA	204

LIST OF ILLUSTRATIONS.

	PAGE
RUBAGA, THE CAPITAL OF UGANDA	*frontispiece*
KING MTESA AND HIS CHIEFS	25
THE HIGHLAND LASSIE LEAVING TEIGNMOUTH HARBOUR	37
DR. JOHN SMITH'S GRAVE AT KAGEI	44
THE C.M.S. FLEET ON THE VICTORIA NYANZA, 1877	53
THE EXTERIOR OF MTESA'S TOMB	97
THE INTERIOR OF MTESA'S TOMB	101
BISHOP HANNINGTON	113
SCENE OF THE FIRST BOY MARTYRS' DEATH	133
BISHOP HENRY PERROTT PARKER	148
MWANGA, KING OF UGANDA	159
THE MISSION STATION AT USAMBIRO	175
ALEXANDER M. MACKAY	189
GOD'S ACRE AT USAMBIRO	200
BISHOP TUCKER AND THE UGANDA MISSIONARIES	207

CHAPTER I.

A CALL FROM AFAR.

'Ethiopia shall soon stretch out her hands unto God.'—PSALM lxviii. 31.

THE existence of the now well-known Victoria Nyanza, the vast inland sea lying 3,300 feet above the level of the ocean, and occupying an area larger than that of Scotland, was first made known to the civilised world by Krapf, the pioneer missionary of East Africa. It had indeed been spoken of some hundreds of years earlier. In the second century the geographer Ptolemy described the Nile as issuing from two great lakes at the foot of the 'Mountains of the Moon.' In the twelfth century the Arab geographer, Aboulfeda, wrote of a lake which he called Koura, lying under the Equator, and extending nine and a half degrees from north to south, from which flowed the three 'Niles,' or great rivers of Africa. Yet, in spite of this concurrent testimony to the existence of a large mass or masses of water in the east central regions of Africa, we find the newly-formed African Association, in 1788, writing of that continent as 'penetrated by no inland seas, nor overspread with extensive lakes, like those of North America; nor having, in common with other continents, rivers running from the centre to the extremities.'

But in the year 1843, the vessel in which Dr. Krapf,

who had been compelled to relinquish his work in Abyssinia, was travelling to Zanzibar, stopped at a port called Takaunga, and here the missionary heard the natives speak of a country in the interior called 'Uniamesi,' where there was 'a great lake.' Krapf continued his voyage to Zanzibar, whence he afterwards returned to Mombasa, and crossing over to the mainland, began work in East Africa by starting, together with Rebmann, a Mission station at Rabai, situated on the hills, fifteen miles up a creek which runs inland from Mombasa harbour. For some years he heard nothing more of the lake. On one of the exploring tours made by the missionaries Rebmann sighted, in the year 1848, the snow-crowned mountain Kilima-Njaro, the discovery of which caused much sensation in geographical circles. In the following year Krapf discovered the snow mountain Kenia, further to the north-west. Two years later, in 1851, when on a journey in Ukambani, he met with a merchant who again spoke to him of the great lake. This man told him of a lake to the north-east of Mount Kenia, and stated that it was connected by a river with a much larger one, which had 'no end, although one should travel for a hundred days to see the end,' and where it was impossible to see across from shore to shore. Still later on, Rebmann obtained further information about it; and in 1855, the year of Krapf's return to Europe, he sent to a German periodical, the *Calwer-Missions-Blatt*, a map of the lake compiled by himself and his companion Erhardt. The map was put together from the details which had been given to the missionaries by traders from the interior.

This curious map of the 'Great Inland Sea of Uniamesi' was copied into the *Church Missionary Intelligencer*. It represents the 'sea' as extending from the Equator to lat. 13° S., extremely narrow at the southern end, making about lat. 10° S. a sudden bend to the westward, and again at lat. 8° S. another bend to the northward, where it attains a width of five degrees. It is thus made to occupy an area equal to that of Lakes Nyassa, Tanganyika, and Victoria, with much of the intervening country. The northern part is called the 'Sea of Ukerewe,' and is pushed some distance to the west of its actual position. There is no mention in this map of any name that might answer to the kingdom of Uganda, and it does not appear that any rumours of such a place had reached the missionaries.

A large map, based on that of Rebmann and Erhardt, was prepared and exhibited at the Royal Geographical Society in 1856. It naturally excited the greatest interest and curiosity, and was the immediate cause of the expedition of Burton and Speke in the following year. These travellers discovered, instead of the monster sea, two lakes, Tanganyika and the 'Sea of Ukerewe,' to which Speke gave the name of the 'Victoria Nyanza' (Nyanza or Nyassa meaning 'sea'). Two years later Lake Nyassa (which had been previously known to the Portuguese) was reached by Livingstone. And in 1861 Speke and Grant together explored the Victoria Nyanza, and discovered the Nile flowing out of it northward. This finally settled the question, so long asked and so long unanswered, as to the original source of the great river of Egypt. It was on this occasion that the first white men visited Uganda, where Speke resided as the guest of King Mtesa from February to July 1862.

In 1874 an officer of Colonel Gordon, then Governor of the Egyptian Soudan, reached Uganda from the north; and in 1875 occurred Stanley's memorable visit to King Mtesa, when the great explorer was making his way through the 'Dark Continent.' Between the visits of Speke and Stanley, Mtesa, who is described by the former as a volatile and frivolous youth, had grown into an intelligent and dignified monarch. He had come under the influence of Arab traders, and had made a profession of Mohammedanism, which he also enjoined on his principal chiefs. The country had made some advance in outward civilisation. Stanley writes :—

'I landed amid a concourse of two thousand people, who saluted me with a deafening volley of musketry and waving of flags. Katakiro[1], the chief Mukungu, or officer, in Uganda, then conducted me to comfortable quarters, to which shortly afterwards were brought sixteen goats, ten oxen, an immense quantity of bananas, plantains, sweet potatoes, besides eggs, chickens, milk, rice, ghee, and butter. After such a royal and bountiful gift I felt more curiosity than ever to see the generous monarch ; and in the afternoon Mtesa sent to say that he was ready to welcome me. Issuing out of my quarters, I found myself in a broad street eighty feet wide and half a mile long, which was lined by his personal guards and attendants, his captains and their respective retinues, to the number of about three thousand. At the extreme end of this street, and fronting it, was the king's audience house, in whose shadow I saw dimly the figure of the king sitting in a chair. As I advanced towards him the soldiers continued to fire their guns. The drums, sixteen in number, beat out a fearful tempest of sound, and the flags waved. Arrived before the audience house the king rose—a tall and slender figure, dressed

---

[1] The traveller mistakes the title of *katikiro*, or chief minister, for the name of the man holding the office.

in Arab costume—approached me a few paces, held out his hand mutely, while the drums continued their terrible noise, and we stood silently gazing at each other during a few minutes. But soon relieved from the oppressive noise of the huge drums and the hospitable violence of the many screaming discordant fifes, I was invited to sit; Mtesa first showing the example, followed by his great captains, about one hundred in number.'

Stanley endeavoured to set before the king the claims of Christianity, and with such success that Mtesa determined to observe the Christian as well as the Moslem Sabbath, and had the Ten Commandments written for him in Arabic on a board, as well as the Lord's Prayer, and the 'Golden Rule,' 'Thou shalt love thy neighbour as thyself.' He further desired to have Christian teachers sent out to him, and the letter from Mr. Stanley conveying this request appeared in the *Daily Telegraph* in November 1875. This letter at once attracted the attention of the Church Missionary Committee.

Three days later the following letter was received by the Lay Secretary of the Church Missionary Society:—

'NOVEMBER 17, 1875.

'DEAR MR. HUTCHINSON,—

'My eyes have often been strained wistfully towards the interior of Africa, west of Mombasa, and I have longed and prayed for the time when the Lord would by His Providence open there a door of entrance to the heralds of the Gospel.

'The appeal of the energetic explorer Stanley to the Christian Church from Mtesa's capital, Uganda, taken in connection with Colonel Gordon's occupation of the upper territories of the Nile, seems to me to indicate that the time has come for the soldiers of the Cross to make an advance into that region.

'If the Committee of the Church Missionary Society are prepared at once and with energy to organise a mission to the Victoria Nyanza, I shall account it a high privilege to place £5,000 at their disposal, as a nucleus for the expenses of the undertaking.

'I am not so sanguine as to look for the rapidity of success contemplated by Mr. Stanley; but if the Mission be undertaken in simple and trustful dependence upon the Lord of the Harvest, surely no insurmountable difficulty need be anticipated, but His presence and blessing be confidently expected, as we go forward in obedience to the indications of His Providence and the commands of His Word.

'I only desire to be known in this matter as

'AN UNPROFITABLE SERVANT.

'(Luke xvii. 10).'

The call to advance into the interior of Africa now seemed unmistakable. It was the hand of the missionary which had first drawn aside the dark curtain enshrouding the country, and shown enough of what lay beyond to tempt the feet of the explorer. Exploration had resulted in a distinct request for teachers of the Gospel. With however little consciousness of what it really meant, Africa was indeed 'stretching out her hands unto God.' The committee felt that this was a call of Divine prompting, and they immediately prepared to obey it. Another gift of £5,000 had quickly followed the first, and in a short time the sum of £24,000 was at their disposal for the undertaking.

The Divine Master had already been preparing the pioneers of the Mission for their arduous task. And in the first offer of service the interests of East and West Africa were blended together in a remarkable way, seeming to point onward to the time when the glad tidings should sound right across the long-forsaken continent, from coast to coast.

The story of little Adjai's rescue from the slave ship in 1822 is well known to the friends of Missions. On board the vessel which was the means of saving the future 'black Bishop' of the Niger was a young midshipman, afterwards Captain Shergold Smith, R.N His son, Lieutenant George Shergold Smith, served in the Ashanti expedition. Here he was employed in the difficult work of securing native porters to accompany the army. The carrying out of this task afforded him some experience of, and insight into, the African character. On a journey taken on this business he caught a fever, which so injured his eyesight that he was recommended to retire on a pension. Returning home, he resolved to devote himself to the ministry of the Gospel, and entered St. John's Hall, Highbury, as a student. Finding his eyesight improve, his thoughts turned again to the country where he had seen the 'gross darkness' covering the people. 'I love the African,' he said, 'and I want to preach Christ to him.' He had already been in communication with the Church Missionary Society when the call came for labourers for the Victoria Nyanza Mission. He at once volunteered for the work. 'Send me out,' he said, 'in any capacity. I am willing to take the lowest place.' But the committee, perceiving the worth of his character and his experience, at once appointed him leader of the expedition.

In the meantime the call had reached another whose

heart 'burned for the deliverance of Africa.' This was Alexander Mackay, a young Scotchman engaged in engineering work at Berlin. His whole bringing up had been a preparation for work among the heathen abroad. The son of a Free Church minister, well educated, trained in various branches of practical knowledge, five years a teacher in Dr. Guthrie's Ragged School in Edinburgh, he had gone to Germany, not merely to work and to distinguish himself as an engineer, but to use every opportunity of diffusing Scriptural truth and of winning souls for Christ. Like Lieutenant Smith, he had already sought an opening for missionary work in Africa, and his offer of service for the Victoria Nyanza followed close upon that of the latter. Once accepted, he used the time that remained to him before starting on the expedition, to fit himself in every possible way still further for whatever might devolve on him to do.

These two men, together with Mr. G. J. Clark, a railway contractor's engineer, were accepted by the committee in January 1876. To them were added Mr. Mr. T. O'Neill, an architect, and the Rev. C. T. Wilson, of St. Mary's Hall, Oxford, curate of Collyhurst, Manchester, who had spent some time in Australia. They were accepted, the one in February, the other in March of the same year. Mr. W. M. Robertson, a skilled artisan, was also accepted in February. The committee were anxious to secure a medical man for the expedition, but had not yet found one, when Mr. Mackay met with a young doctor, then labouring among the poor in Edinburgh, who had been a fellow-teacher with him in the Sunday School, and whose thoughts had been turned towards Mission work in Africa. Dr. John Smith was accepted only half an hour before the instructions of the committee were delivered to five of the party (Lieutenant Smith and the two artisans having already started) before leaving for the field of action. Among the five was Mr. James Robertson, a builder of Newcastle, accepted also at the last moment, who, though unable to obtain the sanction of the Society's medical board, had determined to go out at his own cost and his own risk.

It was at this quiet, yet solemn dismissal, in the old committee room of the Church Missionary House in Salisbury Square, that Mr. Mackay uttered the simple yet memorable words well remembered, and recorded after his own call up higher. 'He was the youngest of the band' (we quote from the *Church Missionary Intelligencer* for May 1890), 'and was called upon last (to reply to the instructions delivered by the Rev. Henry Wright, the Honorary Secretary). "There is one thing," were his words in substance, " which my brethren have not said, and which I want to say. I want to remind the committee that within six months they will probably hear that one of us is dead." The words were startling, and there was a silence that might be felt. Then he went on, " Yes ; is it at all likely that eight Englishmen should start for Central Africa, and all be alive six months after ? One of us, at least—it may be I—will surely fall before that. But," he added, " what I want to say is this : when that news comes, do not be cast down, but send some one else immediately to take the vacant place."'

The whole story of the Victoria Nyanza Mission seems mapped out beforehand in these simple words. It is a story of danger and death, of trial and reverse, of ever-recurring need; but at the same time a story of unflinching courage and enduring devotion, of many a change in the order and aspect of the battle, but of one purpose put forth, clung to, and carried out, under the leadership of One of whom it is written, that 'He shall not fail nor be discouraged.'[1] In no Mission has more heroism been demanded of, and displayed by, the soldiers of the Cross; but at the same time in no Mission has it been more manifest that the work was of God, and not of man. Many have been the places left vacant in the field since the work began, and they have not always been filled up at once. Of the eight who started on the Mission only three ever reached Uganda, and of these three but one is living now; while one only, the man who uttered that note of warning beforehand, was able to remain year after year at his post, and to gather fruit of the seed sown amid loss and tears. Long did Alexander Mackay 'hold the fort' on the shores of the Victoria Nyanza almost alone. True to his parting exhortation, he refused to be 'cast down,' even when prospects seemed blackest, and human help farthest off. And when at length he was called to his rest above, and the mainstay of the Mission seemed removed, then at length the shores of the lake were trodden by fresh footsteps, and the brightness of a new day dawned upon Uganda.

> From forest depths and river strands
>   Where scarce a stranger's foot hath trod,
> Lo! Afric stretcheth out her hands,
>   And seeketh after God.
>
> *We* sought the fountains of the Nile;
>   *She* seeks the everlasting spring,
> The streams that make the desert smile,
>   And health and gladness bring.
>
> She seeks, unknowing what may be
>   The end and object of her quest,
> She asks, yet all unconsciously,
>   For life, and peace, and rest.

---

[1] Isa. xlii. 4.

A CALL FROM AFAR.

Speed forth the word! Too long hath night
 Lain heavy on those regions fair;
Draw back the curtain, that the light
 Of heaven may enter there!

How beautiful on hill or vale,
 By river side or stately grove,
Shall be their feet who tell the tale
 Of Jesus and His love!

God of all goodness, give the word,
 Then swiftly shall Thy heralds move,
And Afric's sons shall own Thee Lord,
 Obey, and praise Thy love!

S. G. S.

CHAPTER II.

A LAND OF DARKNESS.

'Full of the habitations of cruelty.'—PSALM lxxiv. 20.

THE country which the providence of God had in such a wonderful manner brought before the eyes of the civilised world, and from which the call had so distinctly sounded for preachers of the Gospel to 'come over and help,' is one of the most remarkable in the vast continent of Africa. Lying just under the Equator, on the shores of a great inland sea, it has a particularly healthy climate, the temperature rising but little above 80° Fahr., and seldom sinking below 60° at night. The land is a succession of hills and hollows, the scenery being often not unlike that of an English park, and at times singularly beautiful. The hollows often contain swamps, but the hills are covered—or, rather, were so, before the desolating revolutionary wars—with rich groves of plantain and bananas. The soil is exceedingly fertile, and well adapted for cultivation, and there is good pasture land. Travellers who have passed through arid deserts, and made the often perilous voyage across the lake, are apt, when they reach Uganda, to look upon it as a sort of paradise.

A higher degree of civilisation is found here than in most of the surrounding tribes. The Waganda, or Baganda, as they call themselves, are a very intelligent

KING MTESA AND HIS CHIEFS.

race, possessed of many fine qualities. They have considerable manual skill, working well in metals—brass, iron, and copper—and dressing skins beautifully, and they are also great adepts at basket-making. The field work is left to the women. Their clothing is particularly neat. They wear long robes, fastened on the right shoulder, made for the most part of *mbugu*, the inner bark of a fig-tree, beaten out and carefully sewn together. But cotton-cloth and coloured calicoes are also used when they can be obtained. They wear ornaments finely worked in beads, such as necklets and girdles, and ivory bracelets are also found among them. Some of the great chiefs wear robes of scarlet cloth richly embroidered in gold and silver. The snowy whiteness of some of the robes has been a matter of surprise to strangers. The white robe is called *kansu*. A dirty-looking soap is manufactured out of the peelings of plantains, which is said to answer its purpose well.

The huts of the people are made of straw or grass, resting on long poles, and are of a conical shape, like a beehive. The houses and gardens of the great are surrounded by fences made of the tall tiger-grass. The houses are built on the slopes of hills, with the door facing the ascent, and there is a clay ridge in front, to prevent a flood of water from rushing down into the house in rainy weather. The sleeping-place is curtained off with bark-cloth, and bedsteads are used, consisting of a framework of branches, which rests on stakes driven into the ground, and which is covered with fine grass and a mat. A large piece of bark-cloth forms the coverlet. A square is marked off by four logs in the middle of the house for a fireplace, and the cooking-pot rests on three stones.

The ordinary food consists of bananas or plantains but beef and goats' flesh are used also, as well as fish.

The people have, as a rule, two meals in the day. Before eating they wash their hands by having water poured over them, or by using a sort of sponge made from the stem of the banana tree. The meals are taken mostly in the porch, around a space covered with green plantain leaves. The national drink is a cider made from bananas, called *mwenge*.

The mass of the people belong, in common with the other tribes of the lake districts, to the great Bantu family, differing widely from the negroes in habits and language. But the ruling caste appear to have come from the north, and are called *Wahuma*, or, rather, *Bahuma*. King Mtesa boasted that he was a descendant of Ham (whose name he may have heard mentioned by the Arabs), and assured Lieutenant Smith that this remote ancestor lay buried in Uganda. Curiously enough, the herdsmen of Uganda, who are also Bahuma, are the most despised of the population. The Baganda are divided into *kyika*, or clans, each of which is distinguished by the name of an animal, and no person may eat the animal after which his clan is named.

Their government was, in theory, before the advent of the British East Africa Company, an absolute monarchy. By the old law of the country the king could not be succeeded by his eldest son. One of the other sons was chosen by an assembly of the great chiefs. On his election to the dignity of *kabaka*, or emperor, he had to seat himself on an ancient stone throne; this was called 'eating' (taking possession of) 'Buganda.' The unsuccessful candidates were in former times slaughtered. The *kabaka* was the sole authority in the country. He appointed his own chiefs and council, declared war, and disposed at his pleasure of the labours of his subjects and the profits of their industry. The degree of despotism which he exercised depended, of course, somewhat on his personal qualities; and the great chiefs, although nominally subject to his will, did, in fact, exercise a varying influence upon him.

Strange to stay, it has been the custom for two women to bear the title of *kabaka*, as well as the king. These were the queen-mother (*namasle*), and the queen-sister (*lubuga*). The latter was chosen from among the princesses. The former was the king's own mother, or, if she were no longer living, his aunt or some other female relative. The older female relatives of King Mtesa appear to have exercised no little degree of influence over him.

The chief minister is called the *katikiro*. The man who held this office for many years under both Mtesa and Mwanga contrived to obtain a considerable amount of power; in fact, this was shown by his retaining office at the death of the former monarch, contrary to the usual custom. The chiefs next in rank are either lords of the five provinces of Buganda, or fill various posts of trust about the king. The rule used to be that the lords of the provinces spent a part of every year at the capital, to wait on the king, while the remainder was passed in their different spheres of government, where they ruled as petty kings, having the right to exact tribute for themselves, besides what the king's tax-gatherers collected for him. Besides these great lords there are many sub-chiefs of lesser rank, some belonging to the 'upper class' in Uganda, the *bataka*, or hereditary landowners.

The lower class, or peasants, are called *bakopi*. They are generally attached to some master, and have the right to serve whom they please, but have been known to suffer punishment occasionally for the crime of deserting one master for another. The three Baganda who came to England in 1879, as envoys to the Queen from King Mtesa, belonged to this class, though they were passed off on the white men as chiefs.

The military force in Uganda was, in former years, not inconsiderable, though probably far below the numbers at which (forgetting that the population of the country could not be judged by that of the capital) some have estimated it. The soldiers, armed with long spears and wooden shields, followed their chiefs to battle, as in feudal times the serfs followed their feudal lord. The king also possessed a fleet of canoes, commanded by an admiral (*gabunga*).

The strong, settled government of Uganda, the intelligence of the people, and the degree of civilisation attained by them, together with the beauty and fertility of the country, made a very favourable impression on those who visited it. But, just as in the hollows between the smiling hills there lay hidden many a swamp infested by venomous reptiles, so below all the superficial show of excellence there existed a depth of evil and of wretchedness hardly to be surpassed anywhere.

Their very strength and power made the Baganda idle, and instead of applying themselves to developing the resources of their country, they preferred to augment their possessions from time to time by raids upon the weaker tribes surrounding them, burning the villages, slaughtering the people, appropriating the herds of cattle, and carrying off large numbers of women and children into slavery. Every class in Uganda was possessed of slaves, even the *bakopi* or peasants, while a ready sale was always found for them among the Arab traders. It is needless to enter here into the horrors of African slavery, and of the transport of these unfortunate human chattels from the interior to the coast. It is an old but terrible story. And though in Uganda a slave might chance to be well treated and to improve his position, the contrary was often the case. Mr. Ashe relates that on one occasion when a tribe, called the Bakedi, were defeated by the Baganda, the women all chose to die sooner than live as slaves.

But it was not slaves alone who suffered in Uganda. In spite of certain forms of justice, which were scrupulously observed, there was little safety either for a man's property or for his life. The weak were the continual prey of the strong. A single passenger along the high road might at any moment be attacked and robbed of all he had with him, and for a poor man there was no redress. But far worse were the cruelties committed by royal order. Suna, the predecessor and father of Mtesa, not unfrequently ordered a *kiwendo*, or wholesale slaughter of human beings; and Mtesa now and then followed his father's example. At the rebuilding of Suna's tomb, executioners were set to watch all the roads that led to the capital, and capture all who passed that way. Peasants coming to the capital with the produce of their land, unaware of what was going on, fell into the trap set for them. When two thousand captives had been secured, the whole number were mercilessly butchered, as an offering to the spirit of the late king. During Mtesa's illness a similar massacre was ordered, in hopes that it would assist his recovery! And these unhappy wretches were not merely killed, but tortured to death after the most horrible fashion. The punishments, too, not only for real offences, but for anything the king chose to reckon as a crime, were so savage, that the code of Uganda might be said to emulate that of Draco of old, and to be written in blood. On one occasion, for instance, Mtesa issued an order that every man should wear a bead on his wrist, on pain of losing his head, and every woman a bead on her waist, on pain of being cut in half! There being no prisons where criminals could be secured with safety, the minor punishments consisted generally of mutilation, such as cutting off hands, feet, ears, or nose. In cases when the criminal was permitted to ransom himself, he was put in the stocks till the ransom was paid.

And yet many a murder was suffered to take place without any punishment. The case is related of a boy, the son of a chief, who told the king that he was impatient to be a chief himself. 'Well,' was the answer, 'you have only to go and kill your father.' The lad acted on the hint, and actually went about bragging of what he had done. One of Mtesa's own sons was shot by his brother, and the only notice taken of the matter was that the missionaries were summoned to attend the wounded man, and that he was removed some miles off, that he might not die near the palace!

In a few words Mr. Ashe has summed up what were common occurrences during his residence in Uganda:—

'Daily went up the terrible cries of unhappy victims, as they were deliberately hacked to pieces, with strips of reed sharp enough to be used as knives, condemned very often for nothing, or merely for some breach of court etiquette. Frequently furnaces were smoking, in which the agonised bodies of persons innocent of any crime were writhing in slow torture, till death, more merciful than their tormentors, ended their anguish and despair. Sometimes scenes of hideous shame were enacted which make the heart sick to contemplate.'

No wonder he exclaims:—

'What a fearful picture was presented in reality

in that gay and bright-looking palace of pleasure built upon its sunny hill!'

The religion of this beautiful, but dark and unhappy country consisted of a kind of worship of spirits called *lubare*. The Baganda believed in a supreme Creator, whom they called Katonga, but said that he had handed over his authority to the *lubares*, of whom there appeared to be many. Some of them represented various phenomena of Nature, such as the rainbow, the earthquake, the thunder; and the two virulent diseases of Uganda (brought on probably by insanitary conditions), *kaumpuli* (the black plague) and the smallpox, are spoken of as evil spirits. Pre-eminent among the *lubares* was that of the Nyanza, who was supposed to have supreme control over its waters, and whom the seamen and fishermen were wont to propitiate by offerings of fruit thrown into the lake. Great respect was paid to Mukasa, the person in whom the *lubare* of the lake was supposed to reside, and he had the power to prevent any one from landing on the coast until he gave permission. The spirits of the departed (if of any importance) were also called *lubare*, and were believed to reside in certain persons, to whom was given the name of *mandwa*. When a *mandwa* died, another speedily rose up to take his place. These men dressed themselves in white or black goat-skin, and carried a club of crooked wood adorned with iron knobs and bells. They affected strange ways and speech, in order to inspire terror.

Uganda possessed no idols, and apparently nothing that could be called worship, but numerous little temples, or rather huts, studded the roadsides, sacred to some *lubare*, generally with a tree growing close by, on which were hung charms, to propitiate the spirit. Charms made of grass, bark-cloth, and various other things were also hung on the doors, and laid on the threshold of the houses, besides being worn on the person. Besides the *mandwa*, or priests of *lubares*, there were diviners, whose business it was to detect criminals, and another class of diviners, somewhat answering to the augurs among the ancient Romans.

The religion of Islam, introduced by the Arabs, had, when the missionaries reached Uganda, taken no hold on the mass of the people, although it had had an undoubted effect in loosening the hold upon them of their own ancestral beliefs. Its adoption for a time by King Mtesa, which was, as a matter of course, followed by his chiefs, was merely nominal. Yet it proved in after years a formidable opponent to the work of the Gospel.

Such was the country, and such the nation, to whom, in answer to the half-unconscious petition for help, the Gospel was about to be sent. It might have been truly described in the words: 'where Satan's seat is';[1] for there indeed the 'strong man armed'[2] kept his palace, and nothing seemed to disturb his reign. Strangely significant was the name given to it by the Arabs, on account of its distance from the coast, and the perils to be passed through in reaching it—the 'Land of the Grave.' But the hour had arrived when the inhabitants of this 'grave' were to 'hear the voice of the Son of God,'[3] and life was to come into the place of death, life new, irresistible, immortal.

> 'For God is love, and He liveth,
> And life is His living breath,
> And one breath of life is stronger
> Than all the hosts of death.'
>
> *Author of the Schönberg-Cotta Family.*

---

[1] Rev. ii. 13. [2] Luke xi. 21. [3] John v. 25.

CHAPTER III.

FROM THE SHORES OF ENGLAND TO NYANZA.

'He led them forth by the right way.'—PSALM cvii. 7.

THE shortest route to the Victoria Nyanza, reckoned by distance, is through Egypt and the Egyptian Soudan, up the Nile, which issues from the lake at the Ripon Falls, the western boundary of Uganda. It might have been supposed that the Mission party would have been sent by this route. But there were strong reasons against it. It would have involved a journey through the midst of many hostile tribes, and would have connected the missionaries, in the minds of the natives, with the advance of the Egyptian power. The whole series of events which led to the sending forth of the Mission pointed to the route by the east coast as the one to be chosen. Dr. Krapf, who from his retreat in Wurtemberg watched with the keenest interest the progress of the matter, urged the desirability of making the start north-westward from Mombasa, following the line of his own former journeys to Ukambani, and continuing so as to reach the north-western shore of the lake. This was, however, for the most part an unknown route, and it seemed wiser to follow in the track of Burton, Speke, Grant, Stanley, and Cameron, starting from the mainland opposite Zanzibar, and journeying westward in the direction of

Unyanyembe, and thence to the lake. Much valuable advice was given by Colonel Grant; and Lieutenant Cameron, on his return from Africa, also took an interest in the plans of the Society, and offered some important suggestions.

The first start was made on March 11, 1876, when Lieutenant Smith sailed out of Teignmouth harbour in the Highland Lassie, an 80-ton sailing yacht, presented by friends to the East African Mission for service on the coast. Before starting Lieutenant Smith spoke to the crew of Him to whose service both the vessel and its present commander were devoted, and all knelt down together and commended themselves to the care of their great Captain. The Highland Lassie encountered much rough weather on the voyage, but reached her destination without harm on June 20. Lieutenant Smith, however, left her at Aden, under charge of the mate, and, continuing his voyage by steamer, arrived a month earlier.

He immediately proceeded, together with Mr. Mackay, who had travelled by the same steamer, to explore the rivers Wami and Kingani, which, rising in the highlands of Usagara, fall into the sea at no great distance from one another, opposite the island of Zanzibar. It was at first thought that Usagara might be most easily reached by water, but the fallacy of the idea soon became evident. The course of both rivers was so tortuous that the progress of the little steam-launch Daisy, which had been brought out from England, was extremely slow. After difficult navigation up stream for twenty miles the voyagers would find themselves but a couple of hours' distance by land from the point whence they started. Stumps of trees in the channel were, moreover, a frequent source of danger. The rivers wound through banks of dense jungle and

THE HIGHLAND LASSIE LEAVING TEIGNMOUTH HARBOUR.

stretches of slimy, unwholesome plains, where poisonous malaria lurked. Further inland the face of the country improved, and prosperous-looking villages were passed, whence the natives poured out to gaze at their strange visitors; and one chief assured the missionaries that he would be delighted if they would come and stay in his country, and that he would give them the whole of it!

Meanwhile the work of collecting and packing stores, and engaging porters, had gone on vigorously at the coast. By July 1 the whole Mission party were assembled there, and nearly ready for the start by land. They had to take with them on the journey not merely personal luggage, as well as all kinds of articles for the industrial work of the Mission, but also the 'money' for the way, both for the purchase of food, and also for the *hongo*, or tribute exacted of travellers by chiefs through whose territory they had to pass. The 'money' current in the regions for which they were bound consists of cotton-cloth, brass wire, and beads. The whole of the stores had to be carried on men's shoulders, and it took both time and tact to engage the porters necessary for the undertaking. These porters, *pagaazi*, who hire themselves out to travellers, belong mostly to various tribes of the interior. Having come down to the coast in the employ of some merchant or traveller, they are ready to accompany others inland again as far as their own country. It was necessary, however, to secure a certain number of Zanzibar men, as none of the inland *pagaaz* would go the whole of the way.

At length, on July 14, the first division of the party started from Bagamoyo on the coast, followed at intervals by three others, Lieutenant Smith himself remaining to the last. But already the shadow of loss had fallen upon the brave little band, and Mr. Mackay's note of warning was sadly verified. Mr. James Robertson (who had gone out at his own risk) was taken ill shortly after his arrival at the coast, and on August 5, before the last of the band had started, he had entered into rest. The new start for the evangelisation of East Africa, like the first one, was inaugurated by a death. A small limestone pyramid on French Island marks the grave of the first member of the Victoria Nyanza Mission who fell in this enterprise.

The march of two hundred and twenty miles to Mpwapwa, in Usagara, where the first Mission station on the way to the lake was to be founded, was not without its difficulties and trials. It was no easy matter to exercise proper control over the half-savage, self-willed *pagaazi*. There were vexatious delays, owing to the desire of the chiefs through whose countries they passed to detain the travellers awhile, in the hope of making more profit out of them. Then Mr. Mackay speaks of the difficulties occasioned by the 'wild-goose method of marching, which we, like all before us, have adopted.' The path, whether it lay through cultivated field, forest, jungle, tall grass, swamp, or stony ravine, was usually wide enough only for a single traveller, and no one had ever attempted to improve it. Often, in fact, a way had to be cut through the vegetation. Often the march was made through heavy rain; and the party did not escape attacks of fever, while a few of the porters were carried off by small-pox.

The road to Mpwapwa rises gradually from the coast to a plateau 1,500 feet high, to which succeeds the great mountain range of East Africa, reaching here to a height of from 4,000 to 5,000 feet. A descent of 1,000 feet leads to a second plateau, on the edge of which stands Mpwapwa itself, finely situated on the heights, overlooking an extensive plain nearly covered with forest, and abounding in wild animals. It is a fine, healthy situation.

The missionaries were well received by the people of Mpwapwa, and here was commenced the first Mission station on the way to the lake, Mr. G. J. Clark being left in charge of it, together with the mate of the Highland Lassie, who had accompanied the party. The remaining five proceeded towards the lake, Mr. O'Neill and the Rev. C. T. Wilson going on first, while Lieutenant Smith followed with Dr. John Smith and Mr. Mackay.

The second stage of the journey was even more trying than the first. The route led over the Marenga Mkhali, a *pori*, or waterless plain extending forty miles. This crossed, the travellers found themselves in the treeless plains of Ugogo. Here they had to pay heavy *hongo* to the various petty chiefs, who delayed their passage as much as possible, in order to get all they could out of them. The first party passed over a second and longer *pori*, the Mgunda Mkhali, and both met at Nguru, in Usukuma, on the borders of Unyamwezi. Meanwhile their number had been reduced to four, for Mr. Mackay, sorely against his will, had been compelled by the doctor to return to the coast.

At Nguru, the porters, finding themselves in their own country, considered their engagement at an end, and quietly laid down their loads and walked off. Being unable to obtain fresh ones close at hand, Lieutenant Smith proceeded westward to Unyanyembe to procure more. The district of Unyanyembe is an important trading centre, and possessed at that time an Arab governor under the Sultan of Zanzibar. Its principal village or town is Kazeh, or Taboro. Here Lieutenant

Smith was delayed for some weeks, the natives being utterly regardless of the flight of time. Meanwhile Mr. O'Neill and Mr. Wilson had gone on with a small caravan towards the lake, passing through Usukuma, of which Mr. O'Neill gives a pleasing picture. 'The whole distance travelled over,' he writes, 'is studded with villages, nicely situated, and surrounded by green hedgerows of euphorbia; altogether the country is a fine, open one, with much cattle, and well cultivated, every village having a considerable breadth of land sown with Indian corn or millet, and everywhere water is abundant. I should say it would by proper management become a very rich country; but the great drawback is the absence of any king or ruler recognised over the entire country. Kings there are in abundance, for every village we passed had one, but there is no central authority. . . . The people are a mild and industrious race.'

On January 29, 1877, the travellers reached Kagei, on the southern shore of the lake, at the entrance to Speke Gulf. Lieutenant Smith and Dr. Smith did not arrive till April 1, owing to bad health and various troubles. The former writes :—

'Our journey from Nguru to this place was a stormy one. It seemed to me that all Satan's force was allied against us. The men deserted by fifties; lies, thefts, false reports, all were used to delay us, and it took us six weeks to accomplish that which can easily be done in sixteen days. All our marketable cloth was stolen either by our own *pagaazi* or on the highway, and stays of two and sometimes three days at one village during the rainy season, without sufficient protection for our goods, caused us much loss. But He that is stronger was with us, and enabled us to overcome all difficulties, bringing us to this place on April 1. You may

DR. JOHN SMITH'S GRAVE AT KAGEI.

imagine with what joy and thankfulness I first beheld the lake, its blue waters gleaming like a bit of sea in the distance.'

Kagei was the first place on the shores of the lake visited by Stanley, and there the missionaries found the grave of one of his men, with the inscription: 'F. B. 1875. Stanley's Ex.' It was not long before another grave hallowed the place whence the first messengers of the Gospel of peace looked down upon the waters that were to bear them to Uganda. Dr. Smith, who had enjoyed remarkable health for the greater part of the journey, suffered greatly from fever on the last march from Nguru, and was carried the whole of the way. On his arrival at the lake he began to improve, but an attack of dysentery, which he had not strength to resist, proved to be the messenger to summon him to the immediate presence of the Master whom he served. Calmly and peacefully he passed away on May 11, leaving a great gap in the missionary circle. A pile of stones was raised over his grave, with a block of sandstone for a headstone, on which an inscription was cut by Mr. O'Neill; and there that grave stands as a sentinel, watching until the glory of the Lord shall cover the plains around, and shine across the waters that stretch out in front of it, a silent witness for Christ until He come.

The telegram from Aden which conveyed the news home also brought tidings of progress in the work for which that young life had been laid down. It ran thus: 'Dr. John Smith dead. Daisy Nyanza. Mpwapwa road completed.' The little steam-launch Daisy, which had been brought out from England in sections, and put together for the voyage up the rivers Wami and Kingani, had again been taken to pieces for the journey up to the lake. The sections, however, reached Kagei considerably injured and reduced in number, looking, Mr. O'Neill writes, 'a perfect wreck.' The first work was to rebuild her, when six inches more gunwale were added, to increase her seaworthiness, and a false keel, to improve her sailing qualities. The telegram refers to her being finished and launched on the Victoria Nyanza, for which she was originally destined. A pier was also run out a short distance into the lake, constructed with the large stones with which the country abounds, for the convenience of loading and landing goods. It was intended also to build another boat, but there was no timber suitable for the purpose. Lieutenant Smith resolved therefore to visit Ukerewe, where he heard there was a dhow, or Arab boat, which he might be able to purchase.

Ukerewe is a large island on the lake, which was called after it 'Sea of Ukerewe' (as before mentioned). It is twenty-five miles from Kagei. It had been visited before Lieutenant Smith's arrival by Mr. Wilson, the king, Lukongeh, having sent the missionaries a present of sheep and goats, with an invitation to go and see him. During the stormy voyage thither the canoe men kept singing, and one of their songs ran thus: 'Many men are dead; for them we are sorry, for they never saw the white man. We have seen the white man, and are glad.' Lieutenant Smith, in relating the circumstances of his visit, gives the following conversation with canoe men, as an instance of an African's idea of time :—

'When will you take me to Ukerewe?'
'Whenever you like.'
'Then in two hours be ready.'
'No go to-day; to-day must go and sell bananas; go to-morrow.'

Smith was well received by the king, and concluded

the purchase of the dhow with the Arab Songoro, to whom she belonged, little thinking that this man would be the cause of his death and that of his companion, Mr. O'Neill!˙ He wrote from Ukerewe:—

'Now as we are about taking possession in the name of Christ of our respective kingdoms' (it being intended that one party should proceed to Karagwé, the other to Uganda), 'pray for us. How much we need your prayers we ourselves faintly know. Yet this we know: He heareth you.'

In the meantime, Mr. Mackay, who had had to be carried in a hammock the greater part of the way back to Mpwapwa had arrived at the coast with restored health. He was now busy constructing a rough road for bullock waggons from Saadani, a few miles above the mouth of the Wami, to Mpwapwa—no light task to accomplish with only native labourers, utterly ignorant of such work. He engaged forty men (besides donkey men and other supernumeraries), and equipped them with American hatchets, English axes, Snider sword bayonets, picks, spades, and saws. He provided himself besides with carpenters' tools, hammers, one donkey-load of nails and another of cocoa-nut rope, and last, but not least, a small grindstone. 'This,' he writes, ' I have mounted on a wooden frame, and every evening we return from work in time the edges of the tools are applied to the face of this wonderful machine, while the villagers crowd round, as anxiously gazing on as little Toddie ever did when he "wanted to see the wheels go wound."' For a good part of the first fifty miles there was dense jungle to cut through, and here the branches of the trees were so thickly intertwined with the creepers, that to hew a tree by the roots seldom meant bringing it down. Here the Sniders did good work. Then there were *nullahs* or deep watercourses to be passed. Over one Mr. Mackay built a bridge of timber as hard as iron, a great marvel in the eyes of the natives. But this occupied seven days, and as there was not enough time to be expended over the others, a sloping way was made down the bank of the *nullah*, and in some cases it was avoided by a long *détour*. Mr. Mackay thus describes what the natives thought of it :—

'Passers-by open their mouth as well as their eyes at the *njia kubwa* (big road) of the white man; and when they return to talk together at evening in their *tembes* (native dwellings), the story of the "big road" is told; and, as is always the case in Africa, with enormous exaggeration. With the chief men, however, the story does not always go well down; and the report is being widely spread that the English are coming to take possession of the country, an alarm which I hope will die a speedy and natural death. The chief of the village near which I made the bridge took a more practical view of the matter, and told me one day, with all the command his dirty visage could assume, that I must pay him a hundred dollars for cutting down the trees in his territory. I told him that it was he who should give me the hundred dollars, to pay my men for making a bridge which he and his people could not make, but which, as soon as I was gone, he would call his own, and probably levy *hongo* from those caravans which cared to pay him.'

The road was finished in one hundred days, and during that time Mr. Mackay calculated that what with going to and fro, inspecting and ordering, he walked the whole distance, two hundred and fifty miles at least, half-a-dozen times over, besides occasional help from a donkey. But the ground won was not kept possession of by after-comers, and in course of time thick vegetation again covered what had been cleared with so much pains.

In some twelve years not merely the territory between Mpwapwa and the coast, but the whole of the ground traversed by the missionary band, has passed into the possession not of the English, but of the Germans, a possession, it is true, at present in great part merely nominal and theoretical, but destined probably to become thoroughly real and effective in the future.

> Soldier, go—but not to claim
>   Mouldering spoils of earth-born treasure;
> Not to build a vaunting name;
>   Not to dwell in tents of pleasure;
> Dream not that the way is smooth,
>   Hope not that the thorns are roses;
> Turn no wishful eye of youth
>   Where the sunny beam reposes;
>   Thou hast sterner work to do,
>   Hosts to cut thy passage through;
> Close behind thee gulfs are burning—
> Forward!—there is no returning.'
>
>   *Anon.*

CHAPTER IV.

THE GOAL REACHED.

'Neither count I my life dear unto myself.'—ACTS xx. 24.

THE original plan of the Mission included the kingdom of Karagwé, situated on the western shore of the Victoria Nyanza. Karagwé had been visited both by Speke and by Stanley, and although tributary to Uganda, appeared to be a kingdom of some importance, while the mild and friendly character of the king, Rumanika, as described by these travellers, augured well for the establishment of a Mission there. Lieutenant Smith had arranged to proceed thither with Mr. Wilson, and then, leaving the latter in Karagwé, to go on himself to Uganda. But two pressing messages from King Mtesa induced him to change his plan. While on the island of Ukerewe a messenger reached him bearing the following letter, written for the king by a boy brought up in Bishop Steere's Mission School in Zanzibar, whom Stanley had left with the king, that he might teach him:—

'TO MY DEAR FRIEND,—

'I have heard that you have reached Ukerewe, so now I want you to come to me quickly. I give you Magombwa to be your guide, and now you must come to me quickly.—This letter from me, Mtesa, King of

Uganda, written by Dallington Scopion Mufta, April
10, 1877.'

Mufta himself had added these lines :—

'To my dear Sir,—
'I have heard that you are in Ukerewe, and
this king is very fond of you. He wants Englishmen
more than all.—This is from your servant, Dallington
Scopion.'

The messenger who brought this letter was quickly
followed by another, bringing the following :—

'My second letter to my dear Friend Wite Men. I
send this my servant that you may come quickly, and
let not this my servant come without you. And send
my salaam to Lukongeh, King of Ukerewe, and Maduma
Mwanangwa of Kageye, and Songoro.—This from me,
Mtesa, King of Uganda.'

On receiving these letters Lieutenant Smith felt that
the visit to Uganda must not be deferred. Accordingly,
on June 25, he and Mr. Wilson started in the Daisy,
leaving Mr. O'Neill at Ukerewe to complete the building
of the dhow. Being favoured with a fresh breeze they
reached Murchison Bay next evening, and the following
day landed, *en route* for Mtesa's capital. But this
voyage, perhaps the most favourable, as far as wind
and weather were concerned, that any missionary has
made across the lake, had its own record of danger and
injury. Desiring to land the first day in order to cook
their midday meal, the voyagers coasted along the shore
of Ukara, a small island north of Ukerewe, and made
for a 'snug little bay' which they thought would suit
their purpose. They observed, as they drew nearer, a
crowd of natives on the shore, who greeted them with
a musical cry, which they mistook for a note of friendly
welcome. But for the sudden appearance of a rock

ahead they would have run right into the hands of their enemies, but Lieutenant Smith, seeing it, immediately put the boat about. This in all probability saved their lives, for the natives immediately poured upon them a shower of spears, arrows, and stones. Lieutenant Smith was struck in the left eye by a stone, Mr. Wilson received a poisoned arrow in his arm, and two of the men were slightly wounded. The boat was immediately put back, and they were soon out of the reach of further injury. Smith, in great pain and blinded, nevertheless sucked the wound in Mr. Wilson's arm, and much of the poison having passed off in his clothes, he sustained no serious harm; but Smith's eye (the good one, for the right was of little use to him) was irreparably injured. In a private letter giving an account of the event he writes :

'It was a merciful preservation, and I shall ever thank God for putting that rock in our way. . . . Don't blame the natives; they gave us warning not to approach by their war-cry, which I mistook for a note of welcome. Doubtless they thought we were come to attack them. . . . I often wondered, looking at it from a sailor's point of view, why Christ was so often called the "Rock," seeing how fatal to mariners rocks generally are. It is different now.'

From Ukara they struck right across the lake, and next morning sighted land, which proved to be some islands off the coast of Uganda. Proceeding up Murchison Bay, with lovely views on either hand, shortly after sunset they anchored off the coast. The following day messengers arrived from Mtesa to bring them up to the capital Rubaga. They arrived there on Saturday, June 30, and rested the Sunday in the huts set apart for them by the king. Their reception next day is best told in the missionaries' own words.

THE C.M.S. FLEET ON THE VICTORIA NYANZA, 1877.
The Daisy is in the centre, the Dhow on the left, and the Dingy on the right.

THE GOAL REACHED.

Mr. Wilson writes :—

'About 8 o'clock a.m. two of the chief officers came to fetch us. They were neatly dressed in Turkish costume, long white tunics, trousers, and stockings, with red shoes and caps. A few soldiers, neatly dressed in white tunics and trousers, and armed with flint-looking guns, formed our escort, as we climbed the hill on the top of which stands Mtesa's palace. This is a long and lofty building of tiger-grass stems, and is thatched with grass and is extremely neat. In front of the palace are a number of courts, separated from one another by high fences of tiger-grass, and sliding doors between them of the same material. These doors were opened as we approached, and closed behind us. In each court two lines of soldiers, dressed in white, were drawn up, between which we passed.

'Arrived at the palace itself, we entered the central hall, hat in hand, and found all the chief men of the country sitting along each side on wooden stools. All were dressed in Turkish costume, some in black tunics, others in red, and others again in white ones. All rose as we entered, and we were conducted to the upper end of the hall, where the king sat on a chair of white wood, with a carpet before him, the rest of the hall being strewn with dry grass. He was dressed in a black Turkish tunic, white trousers bound with red, white stockings, and he wore red shoes, and had a red cap on his head; he also wore a richly mounted sword. He came down from his throne and shook hands with us, and motioned us to two seats which had been placed for us. We then sat for some time looking at one another till he called one of the messengers he had sent to Ukerewe for us, and bade him narrate our adventures, which the man did in an eloquent speech. Then the letter from the Sultan of Zanzibar was read, and next the Society's letters were presented, and the English one translated into Swahili for the king by Mufta, the boy whom Stanley left to instruct the king.'

Lieutenant Smith continues : 'At the first pause the king ordered a *feu de joie* to be fired, and a general rejoicing for the letter; but at the end, where it was said that it was the religion of Jesus Christ which was the foundation of England's greatness and happiness, and would be of his kingdom also, he half rose from his seat, called his head musician, Tolé, to him, and ordered a more vigorous rejoicing to be made, and desired the interpreter to tell us that this which we heard and saw (for all the assembly were bowing their heads and gently and noiselessly clapping their hands, and saying *Nyanzig* five or six times) was for the name of Jesus.'

The missionaries, however, quickly found out that they had to do with a character changeable as the wind. Lieutenant Smith goes on :—

'The following day we went twice. In the morning it was a full court, as before, and from some cause he seemed suspicious of us, and questioned us about Gordon, and rather wanted to bully us into making powder and shot, saying, "Now my heart is not good." We said we came to do as the letter told him, not to make powder and shot; and if he wished it we would not stay. He paused for some time, and then said, "What have you come for— to teach my people to read and write?" We said, "Yes, and whatever useful arts we and those coming may know." Then calling the interpreter, he said, "Tell them now my heart is good; England is my friend."'

In the evening Mtesa sent for the missionaries again. He told them he had wanted to say something in the morning, but was afraid of the Arabs. He wanted to know if they had brought 'The Book,' and was pleased when they assured him they had, and that they hoped soon to give it him in his own language. Little did he guess what that 'Book' was to accomplish—how it was not only to prove the source of new life to numbers of his subjects, but after his death was to revolutionise his kingdom.

Without delay a piece of ground was assigned to the missionaries, and labourers sent to build them a house. The land, about two acres in extent, was on the slope of a hill opposite the one on which the king's palace stood, with a stream of water flowing below. The house was built of the stems of tiger-grass, with a high roof, thatched with grass, and supported by a number of poles, the partitions and doors of the rooms being made also of tiger-grass. A kind of service was commenced at the palace every Sunday, for which day Mtesa professed a certain respect. The king also began to learn the English alphabet, and expressed his desire that his people should learn to read and write. He also showed a remarkable readiness to receive religious instruction. One day he asked why so many white men were unbelievers in Christ. When told that faith was the gift of God, and that no man could call Jesus the Son of God except through the Holy Spirit, he turned to his people and said, pointing upward: 'All comes from above; all comes from God.'

Lieutenant Smith remained for a month, and then leaving Mr. Wilson to occupy the neat little hut built for them by the king's order, went back to Ukerewe in the Daisy. Here he found Mr. O'Neill still busy with the completion of the dhow. Thence he proceeded to Kagei, and then, sailing up Speke Gulf, he explored the rivers Shimeyu and Ruwana. Returning, he next surveyed Jordan's Nullah, to the west of Kagei.

Writing to the Committee of the Church Missionary Society the report of all he had seen, dated November 2, he concludes with the words :—

'Please give me full instructions as to the Society's wishes concerning expenditure, etc. My former instructions are fulfilled, and I joyfully praise God that by His might and by His strength they have been enabled to be carried out with, I trust, the full approval of the committee. Lord Shaftesbury's parting word, Zech. iv. 6—how true !'

Little did he think that the work appointed for him by his great Captain was almost fulfilled, and his time of rest close at hand. Returning to Ukerewe, he found the dhow (which had been named Chimosi, as embodying in its consonants the initials of the Society, C.M.S.) ready to be launched. But to his surprise the king, Lukongeh, appeared with an armed force, and seizing mast, yard, rudder, and anchor, forbade the removal of the dhow, as it was his property. It then transpired that the Arab Songoro had played the king false, having informed the latter that the white men were finishing the dhow for him, instead of saying that they had bought it from him. Moreover, he had never paid the king for the timber, and had also kept for himself a present sent through him to Lukongeh by the missionaries. The matter was at length adjusted by Songoro's rendering to the king a heavy indemnity. They parted in a friendly manner, the king paying a special visit to Mr. O'Neill, to request him to remain on the island, as all the people loved him, because he said *Watcha sugu* (good-morning) to them. Mr. O'Neill had so endeared himself to the islanders that he was known among them by the name of *Watcha Oneeley* (the good O'Neill).

On November 25 the Daisy and the Chimosi,

containing the Mission party, arrived off Kagei, whence they had to fetch the stores left there. But here the dhow, owing to the ground swell, drifted on to the rocks, and was wrecked. Everything of consequence, however, was rescued, save Lieutenant Smith's Bible. 'The lake,' he remarks, 'has never had so noble a gift before.' On December 4 they started for Uganda in the Daisy. Contrary winds, however, obliged them to put back to Ukerewe; and here they became once more involved in the quarrel between Songoro and the king. As far as could be gathered from the conflicting reports of the natives, Songoro begged the loan of the Daisy, in order to transport a part of his household to the mainland. Attacked shortly afterwards by the king, he fled to the missionaries for protection, and they chivalrously refused to give him up. They were then assailed in their turn, and the whole party slain, except one man, who was made prisoner, and two of Songoro's men, who fled.

Thus fell the two leaders of the expedition (for O'Neill was second in command to Smith)—fell on the very threshold of their enterprise, and yet not before the instructions given them at starting had been carried out, the work of preparation effected, and one missionary, at least, placed at the court of Uganda. Their last words unrecorded on earth, their last moments unwitnessed by any friend who could tell of them, their noble, brave, and gentle spirits went back to God, hailed, doubtless, with joyful acclamations above, but leaving a blank and a silence deeply felt on earth.

Hassani, the native interpreter, who was in charge of the Daisy, and who attempted in vain to recover the bodies, sailed across the lake, and carried the mournful tidings to Mr. Wilson. Meanwhile the two men who escaped remained hid in the bush till the next day, when the Daisy returning, they swam off to her, and being landed at Kagei, carried the news of what had happened to Unyanyembe, whence it was sent on by the governor to Zanzibar, and thence telegraphed to England, reaching the committee on March 19, 1878. It was not long before that Lieutenant Smith had written:—

'Wholesome lines are those you sent—

> "I know not the way I'm going,
> But well do I know my Guide."

Pray for us all, that we may know Him better and better until the perfect day. . . . We are truly in the midst of perils—dangers from within and dangers from without—pestilence and sword and sea.'

His mind appears to have dwelt much upon the 'blessed hope' placed before the believer. Again he writes, after reporting the first troubles with Lukongeh:—

'I am lost in contemplation of that glorious time when Christ Jesus our Lord shall come and take His great power and reign, and am fully persuaded that nothing but such an advent can work so marvellous a change as the subduing of all wills unto His will, the making of all hearts His own. . . . We ask prayer that our hopes, our aims, our desires, may be one— the glorification of our Lord Jesus Christ, and the hastening of His kingdom.

Mr. O'Neill was hoping to return to England shortly, and take his wife back with him to Africa. Although Uganda was the goal he aimed at, he was not unmindful of the island where he had spent so many days. But a few days before his murder he wrote from Kagei:—

'My stay at Ukerewe has not been altogether un-

THE GOAL REACHED.

profitable. I have obtained an insight into the language, which is more or less spoken on three-fourths of the lake shore; and I doubt not that I have made some friends, and prepared the way for the favourable reception of my successor. . . . I candidly trust the Lord will send forth many labourers for this portion of His great harvest.'

But Ukerewe still lacks the presence of those who proclaim the gospel of peace !

The blow that had fallen on the Mission was far more crushing than any which could have been anticipated. Of the eight men originally sent out, two (Dr. John Smith and Mr. James Robertson) had succumbed to sickness, two (Mr. J. W. Robertson and Mr. G. J. Clark) had been compelled by ill health to return home. The hopes of the undertaking seemed centred in the other four. And now the two leaders of the expedition had fallen by the hand of the savage, leaving but two of the eight in Africa, the one alone in Uganda, the other also alone on the road thither, many hundreds of miles between them. Strangely, but brightly prophetic were the words of Dr. Krapf written to the committee but a few weeks before the sorrowful news reached Europe :—

'Many reverses may trouble you, but you have the Lord's promises. Though many missionaries may fall in the fight, yet the survivors will pass over the slain in the trenches, and take this great African fortress for the Lord.'

And among the many whose hearts were stirred by the martyr-death of the devoted missionaries was one who was hereafter to lay down his own life as a witness to Africa's need, and as a precious seed-corn, out of which the Lord of the harvest made the abundant fruit to spring forth, the noble Bishop Hannington.

'Ye shall be sorrowful.' The conflict rages
   Between Christ's servants and the hosts of sin,
And ever thus, throughout the passing ages,
   His soldiers fall, unfading crowns to win.

And fall they while the goal still distant lies,
   With scarce a word yet spoken for their Lord,
His sweet approval He doth yet accord;
   Their 'feet' are beauteous in their Master's eyes.

S. G. S.

CHAPTER V.

SOWING THE SEED AMID DIFFICULTIES.

'The seed is the word of God.'—LUKE viii. 11.

WE must now go back to the solitary missionary at the court of King Mtesa. A house of tiger-grass had been erected for the white men about a mile from the palace. The king was fairly friendly, and seemed anxious to learn all that Mr. Wilson could teach him. Regular services were held at the palace on Sunday mornings, when the king hoisted his 'flag,' a 'nondescript thing, consisting of pieces of red, blue, and white calico sewn together.' Passages of Scripture were read in Kiswahili, and explained by Mr. Wilson, Mtesa translating what was said into Luganda, for the benefit of those unacquainted with the former language. In these early days the king showed wonderful readiness to receive the word, and seemed at times thoroughly impressed by it. On one occasion, after Mr. Wilson had been speaking of the power of Christ to save, and urging his hearers to come to Him at once, while there was time, the king took up the word, and 'spoke most eloquently to them, telling them to believe in Christ now, saying they could only do so in this life; when they were dead it would be too late.' *And yet he never came himself!*

Troubles arose from time to time, owing to jealousy

of the foreigner on the part of the chiefs, and also to the Arabs, who had a monopoly of the ivory trade at the court of Uganda, and who feared that the influence of white men would be to their detriment.

Meanwhile, the three months during which Lieutenant Smith expected to be absent passed away, and still Mr. Wilson received no tidings of his brethren.

On November 21, 1877, he writes: 'As this has been my first experience of living in solitude, I have felt rather lonely at times, but lately I have had good company in the shape of five months' letters and papers, which Smith forwarded to me by an Arab, who, however, took them up to the palace instead of bringing them to me, and I have had the greatest difficulty in getting them from the king, having had, as it were, to drag them, one by one, from him. He has a number yet, and when I shall get them I don't know.'

And again on December 22: 'I am still alone, and have no news of Smith and O'Neill, and expect I shall have a solitary Christmas. I am beginning to get a little alarmed about them, as Smith has been away so much longer than he intended.'

He was, moreover, in great need of clothes, having brought but little baggage from Ukerewe, and had to 'tax his tailoring skill' to make himself look respectable. His money, too, or at least such as passed current in Uganda, was gone, and Mtesa supplied him but scantily with food.

At length, on December 31, the sorrowful tidings were brought him by Hassani that his brethren had been murdered. In a couple more days he had started for Kagei, accompanied by some men sent by King Mtesa to ascertain the truth of the story. The voyage was a perilous one, violent storms alternating with dead calm, and it took eight days to reach Kagei.

Here Mr. Wilson met the only survivor of Lieutenant Smith's party on the island, the carpenter Sisamani, who confirmed the story told by Hassani. After repairing the Daisy, Mr. Wilson started for Unyanyembe, to purchase fresh cloth and beads, as there was hardly anything among the stores at Kagei which he could use as 'money.' He hoped also to meet Mr. Mackay, but was disappointed in this, as the latter had been hindered in his advance to the lake. The journey was altogether a trying one, and he arrived back in Uganda towards the end of March in somewhat impaired health. Another five months had yet to elapse before he grasped the hand of the only one of the original party of eight who still remained in Africa.

In the meantime four new labourers had been appointed to the Mission. Two artisans, named Sneath and Tytherleigh, were sent out for the Nyanza, and Dr. Baxter, with Mr. Copplestone, to take possession of Mpwapwa. Mr. Mackay having completed his road to Mpwapwa, returned to the coast, where he found Sneath and Tytherleigh. The former, however, had hardly arrived when he became so ill that he was ordered back to England. The latter rendered great assistance to Mr. Mackay, who now put into execution his plan of transporting the stores wanted for the interior by bullock-waggons to Mpwapwa. The task was not an easy one, but Mr. Mackay decided that it was both easier and more economical than employing a large caravan of porters. Tytherleigh was joined by Mr. Copplestone, while Mr. Mackay was marching to and fro, ordering and arranging all that went on, with unflagging activity and perseverance. Receiving letters from Mr. Wilson, however, urging him to hasten forward, he started off, leaving the others to follow, and proceeded by a route yet untraversed by missionaries. Passing over the Mgunda Mkhali, just then a gigantic swamp which it took a fortnight to wade through, he at length reached Uyui, some thirty miles north-east of Unyanyembe. Here his spirit was greatly stirred by what he saw of the slave-trade. 'Arab caravans,' he writes, 'with tusks of ivory are moving down to the coast now; and each has, as a supplement, a string of living little ones trotting on, with their necks linked together, to be disposed of to the highest bidder at the coast.' Here, also, he learned with deep concern from some men who brought letters from the coast to the Arab governor, of the death of William Tytherleigh, who had received an internal sprain, when helping to push one of the waggons up a hill. This was a great loss to the Mission, and Mackay, writing later on from Uganda, says: 'Oh for Tytherleigh among us! If you can find another Tytherleigh in all England, please send him out; but his like is not to be every day met with.'

On June 12, 1878, Mr. Mackay first sighted the Victoria Nyanza. He writes thus: 'As eagerly as ever the ten thousand Greeks shouted "Thalassa! Thalassa!" in the immortal *Anabasis* of Xenophon, did I gaze on the silvery sea, and thank God that now I was near the Nyanza at last. For had I not been two years and more on the way from the coast to Kagei, and now an end to miserable marching was come, at least for a time? Had not my companions succumbed to the climate one by one, and even reinforcements failed? Now I was here alone, to hold the fort till better days should dawn.'

Mr. Wilson, on reaching Uganda, had sent the Daisy back to Kagei under Hassani. Mr. Mackay found the vessel in great need of repair, and this work, together with the putting in order of the stores left here under charge of native servants, occupied some time. While staying here he resolved to pay a visit to Lukongeh, at Ukerewe, having heard that the king desired a conference with him. His men urged him not to go, saying Lukongeh would certainly put him to death; and finding they could not deter him from his purpose, declined to accompany him. He went alone, with the exception of an interpreter given him by Kaduma, the friendly chief of Kagei, leaving his arms behind, to show that his visit was one of peace. Lukongeh received him well, and expressed sorrow for the murder of Smith and O'Neill, making out that the matter was not his fault. Returning to Kagei, Mackay was greeted with great joy by the natives, who had hardly expected to see him alive again; but, alas! his own men, settling it in their minds that he was murdered, had consumed all his provisions; and the native food, to which he was obliged to have recourse, brought on an illness which detained him some time longer.

At length Mr. Wilson arrived once more at Kagei, expecting to find there a caravan under charge of a native. Instead of that, he tells us: 'The people of Kagei crowded round the canoes as we landed in the dim twilight of the evening, and, on my asking for news, told me a white man had come. In another minute Mackay appeared with a hearty welcome. He, too, had been alone for a long time. We had seen but little of each other before, but as we talked that night of all that had passed in those two years, of those who had fallen, of the reinforcements (come, too, only to die) which had been, or were to be, sent, of our hopes and fears, and plans for the future, it seemed as if we had known each other intimately for years; hour flew by after hour unheeded, weariness was forgotten, and the cocks began to crow, and grey dawn appeared in the east, before we were even conscious that it was growing late.'

The two survivors of the original party started for Uganda on August 23. The Daisy was wrecked on the voyage, but the party were hospitably sheltered by the natives of Usongoro, and after eight weeks spent in repairing the vessel, they once more set sail, and shortly after reached Uganda. Mtesa received them cordially, and gave them a packet which had been sent on by Dr. Emin Effendi (Emin Pasha), containing, besides other things, the welcome tidings that three more missionaries were on their way to the country.

The news of the deaths of Smith and O'Neill had called forth for the Nyanza Mission three volunteers from the Church Missionary College, Mr. Pearson, Mr. Litchfield, and Mr. Hall. It was resolved that these three, together with Mr. Felkin, a young surgeon who had already prepared to join the Mission, should start at once; and this time the (geographically) shorter route by way of the Nile was chosen, Colonel Gordon, then Governor of the Egyptian Soudan, promising to do all in his power to assist them on the journey. Mr. Litchfield was ordained before starting. The party went by steamer from Suez to Suakim on the Red Sea, and at once prepared to cross the desert to Berber, whence they were to proceed up the Nile to Khartoum. But the intense heat, 98° to 100°, struck down one of their number, Mr. Hall, and he was compelled, most reluctantly, to return home. The others, after a trying journey, reached Berber in safety, whence an Egyptian steamer conveyed them to Khartoum. Here they were hospitably received and entertained by Colonel Gordon, who sent them on in one of his steamers. The voyage, though undertaken under these favourable circumstances, was not unattended with trouble and danger. The Bahr-el-Zeber, as the river is called after its junction with the Bahr-el-Abiad (White Nile), was much encumbered with floating islands and immense masses of vegetation, large quantities of land having been detached by the floods and carried northward. This so retarded their progress, that the voyage from Khartoum to Shambeh, which ought to have taken fourteen or fifteen days, occupied sixty-eight, and they were seriously inconvenienced with respect to food. After leaving Gondokoro they had to take to small boats, to pass through the rapids, and the current being very strong, and the river high, the passage was extremely hazardous. From Bedden to Dufli they had to march overland. Thence a steamer conveyed them up to and across the Albert Nyanza, as far as Magungo, where the Murchison Falls intervene. The next stretch of road was almost impassable, now through high grass, which, when one man passed through it, swung back on the next with considerable violence, now over trees and creepers stretching across the path, now through unwholesome swamps. Mr. Litchfield and their dragoman were both attacked by fever, to which the latter succumbed. He passed away peacefully, expressing his trust in Christ. To add to this, the attitude of the natives was most threatening, and their own porters were not to be depended on. At length they were met by Mr. Wilson, who had set off immediately on receiving news of their approach. The journey from Foweira to Mruli, the last of the stations then under the Egyptian Government, was made by boat, and thence they were escorted to Uganda by messengers from King Mtesa, and arrived February 14, 1879.

During Mr. Wilson's absence Mr. Mackay had

carried on the weekly 'service' on Sundays, reading and explaining the Scriptures in Kiswahili, which the king translated into the language of Uganda. Further, Mtesa, who had at first been too jealous to allow his subjects to learn to read, for fear they should outstrip himself and his chiefs, now withdrew his prohibition, and old pupils and young swarmed around Mackay, eager for instruction. Two workshops sprang up on the Mission premises, made of wickerwork, plastered with clay, which excited great admiration. Bullock training was commenced, Mackay having offered to build a carriage for the king, which these animals were to draw. The idle Waganda were astonished to see the white man at work, making a broad road through his *shamba* (garden or plantation). Mtesa at this time showed much interest in the Word of God, and forbade any labour on Sunday. He further, after hearing a lecture from Mackay upon the human body, and a protest against such a piece of workmanship being sold for a rag of cloth, actually forbade the sale of slaves! He also despatched canoes across the lake to Kagei to fetch the men who were believed to have arrived to reinforce the Mission. These were Messrs. Sneath, Penrose, Stokes, and Copplestone. But Mr. Sneath had been again invalided home, and Mr. Penrose, an artisan, had been attacked and slain by *ruga-ruga* (robbers), while conducting a caravan to the lake, thus making the sixth who had fallen since the Mission began.

By the arrival of Messrs. Stokes and Copplestone the party in Uganda was increased to seven—a larger number of Church Missionary Society missionaries than have been there at any subsequent period till the arrival of Bishop Tucker and his party in December 1890. But opposition was not slow to arise. On

February 23, 1879, a party of French Jesuit priests arrived from Algiers, sent out by the Society of Notre Dame d'Afrique, under the then Archbishop of Algiers, now Cardinal Lavigerie. The presents they brought for the king were exactly of such a nature as to please him, including guns, swords, and gunpowder. They immediately took up a position hostile to the Church Missionary Society missionaries, refusing to kneel for prayer at their Sunday services, and denouncing them to the king as liars, who taught a false religion. Mr. Mackay endeavoured to show the king the principal points in which their teaching differed, appealing to the 'Book' for judgment as to which was right; but Mtesa was sorely perplexed, and the chiefs remarked that 'Every white man has a different religion.' Not long after some messengers from Zanzibar brought a letter to the king from the British Consul there, Dr. (now Sir John) Kirk. This letter was mistranslated to the king by the Arabs, who were sworn enemies of the Mission, and made to appear as though it cast reflections both on the character of the missionaries and their honesty of purpose. A very trying time followed for them; the king's manner towards them changed, and he often refused to see them. One day, hearing that the French priests were ill, Mackay and Litchfield set off with some medicine to visit them, little thinking into what danger they were running. Mr. Felkin thus describes the occurrence :—

'As they went by the palace a man came to them, and told their boys that if they went to the Frenchmen they would all get tied up. They thought nothing of this, and went on their way, but soon saw armed men rush past them, and in a short time were brought to a standstill by some thirty or forty men, dancing and brandishing their spears and clubs. They were told to go forward, and at once were surrounded. Mackay saw that they were in great danger, and instantly sat down, calling on Litchfield to do the same, as this is the only chance, it seems, with natives. They then asked what was the meaning of it all, and were told it was the king's order. "Then we will go to the king," Mackay said. When they reached the palace they sent in to say they must see the king at once. No answer was returned, and after waiting a due season, they left.'

Later on, after a visit to the palace, they heard that the soldiers were desirous to kill them, and only waited the king's orders to do it. But however Mtesa's mind may have been poisoned against them by Arab influence, he had a strong reason for not proceeding to extremities, as he was suffering much in his health, and was receiving medical attention from Mr. Felkin. In spite of this, the situation became more and more trying and embarrassing, and the missionaries found it even difficult to obtain food for their daily need. Under these circumstances they proposed to withdraw from the Mission for a time, and requested permission from the king to leave. This, however, he was unwilling to give; but at length he recurred to his intention, already conceived, of sending an embassy to Queen Victoria with one of the missionaries. Three men, by name Namkadi, Kataruba, and Sawaddu, were chosen for this purpose, and in May they started on their journey, under the guidance of Mr. Wilson and Mr. Felkin. Of their journey to and sojourn in England, where much kindness was shown them, and their reception by the Queen, we need not speak here. As far as can be seen, the event was barren of any permanent results, and Namkadi afterwards distinguished himself by his enmity to the missionaries and to their work.

The Church Missionary Society Committee having sanctioned the occupation of Uyui as a Mission station, it was thought best that Messrs. Stokes and Copplestone should return thither and commence work. Mr. Pearson accompanied them as far as Kagei, whence it was needful to fetch some stores; and meanwhile, from June to November 1879, Mackay and Litchfield were alone together in Uganda. A sudden change came over Mtesa's attitude towards them, and these few months were full of encouragement.

Mr. Litchfield wrote : 'Peace is upon us, and there is a wonderful change from the days of our troubles here; in fact, it is like clear sunshine after storm. Mtesa is now taking up the question of education in earnest, and is ordering all his chiefs, *Batongole* (officials), pages, and soldiers, to learn the alphabet, etc., in English characters. Mackay and myself are never free from learners, some of whom are waiting with the daylight. We have our hands full of work to supply them with brain food, and the small printing-press sent out with us from England is in daily requisition. . . . Mackay and myself are now on visiting terms with every chief in the capital without an exception, and not a day passes without our house being filled with visitors. You can think how all this cheers our hearts, and makes us praise Him who has wrought this change. In medicine, too, there has been some progress, as last month's journal shows over two hundred cases, most of which are cures.'

And again he gives us the following interesting glimpse of his 'home' and daily life : 'I have built myself a house—the floor is the earth, the walls tiger-grass, the roof thatch, with three rooms, and lock and key doors. 1st room, reception hall, dispensary, school-room, and hospital; 2nd, storeroom and kitchen; 3rd, *sanctum sanctorum* and bedroom. I battered the floor smooth with a wooden log, and cut holes in the wall for windows, and now it is A1, *ne plus ultra*. Between July and December 1879 I was very busy building, digging, trench-making, road-levelling, planting, printing, dispensing, teaching, translating, making a vocabulary, learning the language, washing, ironing, brick-making, candle-making, and a host of other light and trifling tasks. You would not have known me in the dirty-fisted, clayey individual I was. More than fifty men and boys came daily for instruction to me, and I had taken part through St. John's Gospel, and we were finishing 1 Kings.'

And in his journal we find the following touching entry: 'Went, as I had promised, to see my patients at Monoculia's[1] house. As this chief seemed anxious to talk on religion, I tried to explain the death, resurrection, and love of Christ to him in my poor, broken, stammering language. After a while he went out and sent a slave to fetch me. I went to him and found him in a very small hut on his knees, and he asked me to pray. I said I did not know Swahili, but he said, "Pray in English; God understands you." And I did so, deeply moved by the scene.'

Again he describes a service held in Mtesa's house, and says: 'The king seemed to take a great interest, and translated faithfully for his chiefs. He reminded me of a father surrounded by his children, more than a king by his subjects. His pages sat around his bed, and it was difficult to think we were in the centre of Africa amongst a savage nation.'

The king even asked for baptism; but he could not comply with the conditions necessary to its being granted. With all the undoubted fine qualities of

[1] We shall hear of this man later on, under the name of Isaya.

which he was possessed, and the evident hold which the Word of God for a time obtained upon him, his history is a sad illustration of the words: 'How hardly shall they that have riches enter into the kingdom of God,' and 'If any man love the world, the love of the Father is not in him.'

And the missionaries had yet to wait before one ripe ear should be gathered of the precious seed sown early and late.

> 'We must leave it for a while,
>   The seed which we have sown;
> The spring-tide will not smile
>   Until wintry months have flown:
>
> *   *   *   *   *
>
> Yet not seeing, we believe
>   In a word which cannot die;
> Our times with God we leave;
>   We must wait till by-and-by.'
>
> *Author of 'Copsley Annals.'*

CHAPTER VI.

THE SEED SPRINGING UP.

'I have planted, Apollos watered; but God gave the increase.'—
1 COR. iii. 6.

HITHERTO the hindrances to missionary work in Uganda had arisen partly from the enmity of the Mohammedans, partly from the capricious character of the king, partly from the adhesion to old customs by the chiefs and people, and partly also from the contrary influence brought to bear on Mtesa by the Romish priests. But in the beginning of the year 1880 another foe rose up to dispute the claims of the Gospel of Christ. This was the *lubare* of the lake.

It has been already mentioned that the religion (if such a name may be applied to it) of Uganda consisted mainly in a superstitious reverence of various *lubares* or spirits, who were supposed to reside in the persons of living men, and who had to be propitiated by charms and offerings. The most venerated of these was the *lubare* of the lake, concerning whom Mackay thus wrote in January : 'For several months I have found the word *lubare* more or less in every one's mouth. Many spoke the name with awe, while others refused to say anything good or bad of such a being. At last I learned that the *lubare* was really a spirit, but was personified in an individual—an old woman—who lives on the lake. Month after month a lot of half-caste traders have been trying to get away to Unyamyembe, but each time they went to find canoes they returned to the capital. It appeared that the *lubare* was about to pay a visit to this quarter, and no communication was to be allowed on the lake till the spirit returned home.'

This same *lubare* had hindered Mr. Pearson's landing in the usual place on his return from Kagei, and compelled him to take a long and circuitous route instead. Mukassa, as the witch was called, was now coming with a train of followers to the capital, and was expected to cure the king of his sickness, and presents of food, cattle, etc., were sent to her on the road. Mackay felt that this was a sad return to heathenism on the part of the king, and day by day endeavoured to show him the folly and wickedness of such a course. Such was his zeal that he earned for himself the title of Anti-Mukassa, 'which, however,' he says, 'has no reference to a sofa cushion!' Mtesa now agreed with, and now turned a deaf ear to Mackay's arguments and appeals; and the chiefs, although many of them had been sufficiently enlightened to see the folly of Mukassa's claims, supported her coming to the capital. The matter was pressed on the king by his female relatives, particularly the *namasole*, or queen-mother, and he told his chiefs that they would now leave both the Arab's and the *muzungu's* (white man's) religion, and go back to the religion of their fathers. This announcement apparently gave great pleasure to all. But Mackay wrote:—

'To-day the chiefs followed each other like sheep, yet I am convinced that several present would have chosen quite the contrary, were they not afraid of each other. . . . I do not feel discouraged, only disappointed for the time. No power can stand against that of the cross of Christ.'

In the court of the palace three huts were erected,

one for the *lubare* Mukassa, the others for the representatives of two other deities or spirits. A noisy procession passed up the road to the palace, and the *lubares* were received by the king with all honour. Nothing, however, came of their visit, save the consumption of an enormous amount of native beer. The *lubare* Mukassa was said to have predicted war in the country from the presence of strangers—not immediately, but within four or five years. 'I am sure,' wrote Mackay, 'Mtesa will feel much ashamed of last week's performance.'

Then the tide, which had set strongly against the missionaries, turned again in their favour. The chiefs became friendly once more, and pupils returned. And we find Mtesa himself saying to his subjects, 'Why are you not continuing to learn to read? You are all trying only to gather riches for this world. You had better prepare for the world to come!'

In June 1880 it became evident that the state of Mr. Litchfield's health would no longer permit him to remain in Uganda, and he had to say farewell to the work, in which, despite its trials and difficulties, he had found much to rejoice his heart. The good seed had been carefully and prayerfully sown, and though as yet there was no distinct case of conversion, he could tell of the readiness of the 'common people,' as of old, to hear the good tidings, and of 'numbers of instances where the hearers had testified their astonishment and joy at the love of Jesus in dying for them.' He removed to Uyui, where he remained for some time working with Mr. Copplestone, whom he found just recovering from an attack of fever. Mr. Mackay had accompanied him thither, in order to obtain supplies. In returning he was detained for some time at Kagei, being unable to obtain canoes for the voyage.

It was now Mr. Pearson's turn to be alone in Uganda, and a time it was, not merely of loneliness, but of trial and privation. The king now took another turn, and professed himself a Mohammedan. Mr. Pearson says :—

'He had a dream, and saw ten moons with another moon larger and brighter than the rest, which went on waxing until it had attained an enormous size. The ten moons then came and paid homage to it. While Mtesa was wondering what this meant, two heavenly messengers appeared to him, and with a look of anger, which made him terrified, demanded why he had ceased to say "Allah Akbar," ordering him, if he wished to retain his prosperity, and see his country increase, to return to his old custom, and cry "Allah Akbar" every day, as directed by the Koran.'

Mtesa then ordered all his court to say 'Allah Akbar,' and repeat their Mohammedan prayers in the place that had been used for Christian services. He also gave up hoisting his flag and having a gun fired off on Sundays, the things, writes Mr. Pearson, 'in which his Christianity consisted.'

As a natural consequence the missionary found himself neglected ; and despite the medical and surgical services he was constantly rendering to one and another, he was often in want of the necessaries of life. He writes in July :—

'I have the greatest difficulty in procuring food. I have a very small quantity of shells (cowries) left, and no cloth. Clothing has gone, one article after another (for the purchase of food), until now the question becomes serious. Occasionally I have a few bananas sent me by a chief, but this is rare. Some of the sweet potatoes which I planted have come up, and given us a meal or two. . . . For one or two days we were in great straits, but the good Lord sent enough. Mufta asked Mtesa for some of the shells owing to me. He promised to send them, but after waiting and hungering some days, he went again, and told the king if he did not send me some food or something to buy food with, I and my boys would be found dead. This frightened him, and he sent 2,000 cowries, adding that he would send all when his wife, who had charge of the shells, came home. Chambalango, whom I had attended, as well as one of his wives, sent me a goat and a few bunches of bananas, upon learning the destitute state that I was in. One of the native workmen whom I had taught a few things brought me a goat. Two other goats came from the *katikiro* for repairing and re-silvering two mirrors. I simply placed my destitution before the Lord, and He sent me food in a most marked, unlooked-for manner. To Him be all the glory!'

For some days Mr. Pearson was occupied in putting up a flagstaff for the king, in which work he was hindered and thwarted by a jealous official. At length he was successful, and Mtesa was much pleased. 'I reached home,' writes Pearson, 'very late, tired out, every bone aching. Queer missionary work!'

But he was not without encouragement. Two boys, Luta, son of a chief, and Mukassa, the keeper of the 'church' or 'mosque,' came often to learn from him. The latter refused to go to the Mohammedan prayers when the chiefs went, and said that the religion of Jesus, which the white man taught, was the only true religion, all others being lies. And now came the first beginning of religious persecution: the bold lad was put in the stocks; and shortly after he and Luta were both seized and sent off bound to the country. And Mr. Pearson writes:—

THE SEED SPRINGING UP.

'Alas! now I have no scholars. The interdict is still upon our teaching, and no one comes since Luta and Mukassa were taken off. Lord, clear the way. Give me an open door. Do Thou indeed enable us to light Thy candle in Uganda, which shall never be put out.'

How fully has this prayer been answered!

At length Mr. Mackay reappeared in Uganda, having obtained a passage from Kagei in the boats sent by the king to fetch a fresh company of Romish priests. He found Mtesa, who had heard of the kind reception given to his chiefs in England, purposing to go thither himself; and even appointing Namasole, the queen-mother, to reign in his absence. This plan being given up, he insisted on the missionaries obtaining a daughter of Queen Victoria to be his wife!

Then followed a fresh trouble. Some Arabs, newly arrived from the coast, made up a wicked tale about Mr. Mackay, and told the king that he was an insane murderer who had fled from England, that in Zanzibar he had committed more murders, that he had tried to shoot the Governor of Unyanyembe, and that he had been on his knees to them, to implore them not to reveal his crimes to the king! This was repeated to the missionaries by the French priests, who heard it at *baraza* (the court). Whatever Mtesa may have thought of the story, it suited his purpose to affect to believe it; for though not willing to part with the Englishmen who were so useful to him, he did not want their religion, and he wanted to keep in favour with the Arabs, who hated them.

Mr. Mackay writes: 'We can now understand to the full the meaning of that blessing which we are promised when men shall revile us and persecute us, and shall say all manner of evil against us falsely, for

His sake. We are His, and it matters not what man can do to us.'

But the return of the Baganda envoys from England, accompanied by Mr. Stokes and the Rev. P. O'Flaherty, caused the tide to turn again for awhile. They arrived in March 1881. Mr. O'Flaherty gained considerable influence with Mtesa, and from his knowledge of the Koran was enabled to meet the Arabs on their own ground and confound them. In June the interdict on the foreigners' teaching was removed; crowds again flocked to the missionaries, and their work went on vigorously.

And now the time drew on when the missionaries' hearts were to be gladdened by the sight of precious fruit from the patient seed-sowing of five years. During the time that Mr. Mackay was alone in Uganda, while Mr. Wilson went to meet the Nile party, he had taught a lad named Sembera to read; he was a slave of one of the chiefs, the same who had begged Mr. Litchfield to pray with him. He was most diligent in learning, and in time read through one or two Gospels, the Acts, the Books of Kings, and many Psalms, besides one or two Epistles (in Kiswahili). He had been allowed by his master to accompany Mr. Mackay to Uyui, and was of great assistance to him on the journey. On his return, he was away for some time with his master in a distant part of the country; but was now and then able to visit the missionaries.

Mr. Mackay writes on October 8, 1881: 'To-day he (Sembera) brought me a note written by himself, and very legibly, although he has never had a lesson in writing—written in Luganda, with a pointed piece of spear-grass and some ink of dubious manufacture. It ran thus, " Bwana Mackay, Sembera has come with compliments, and to give you great news. Will you baptize him, because he believes the words of Jesus Christ?" He says he does not fear any danger of being caught and killed, should he be baptized. Mr. O'Flaherty has had a long talk with him, and promises to baptize him by-and-by. To my knowledge his life is exemplary, and his understanding and reception of Christian truth very good for his limited opportunities.'

But before this convert was enrolled among the members of the Church militant, another, unknown at the time, entered the company of the Church triumphant. The story is given in Mr. Mackay's journal:—

'Not long ago there died one of the lads who had been reading with Mr. O'Flaherty. He was ill, and for a while we missed him; then we heard that he was dead. His name was Dumurila, being lame of a foot, and slave of Mongobya. He used to show great eagerness, not only to learn to read, but to become acquainted with the truth itself. . . . The other day, when waiting in the court precincts, Mr. O'Flaherty was accosted by a lad, who handed him a Swahili Gospel, saying that it was given him by Dumurila, to return to the *muzungu*. This lad's story was most affecting. He said that he used to be a most ardent follower of the *lubare*, but he had recently come to leave his old superstition, and in proof of what he said, he showed Mr. O'Flaherty that he had no longer any charms about him. He continued that his friend Dumurila had asked him to come to us for medicine, but he was afraid, as he did not know us. The sick lad had assured him that we would certainly either go to him or send him medicine. All day long he read in the Gospel which he had (St. Mark), and when he found himself in so much pain that he expected to die, he charged this lad to bring back the Gospel to Mr. O'Flaherty without fail. He then asked the *lubare* lad to go and fetch some water from a pool near. When the water was brought he bade his companion sprinkle some on his head, and name over him the names of the Father, the Son, and the Holy Ghost. Soon after that he died. I do believe that this baptism by a *lubare* lad has been written in heaven. It seems to have much moved the lad who told the story, for he professes to have lost his faith in the *lubare*, . . . and wishes to come to learn to know the Book of Jesus Christ. . . . The Word of God takes root where least expected, and brings forth riper fruit than our unbelieving hearts had looked to see.'

On March 18, 1882, Sembero Kumunba, with four other lads, were received into the visible Church of Christ by baptism. The former received the name of Mackay. Another of the five was Mukassa, the lad who had been keeper of the church, or mosque and who was put in the stocks, and afterwards bound and sent into the country, for saying that Christianity was the only true religion. He received the baptismal name of Filipo (after Mr. O'Flaherty). The others were named Henri Raiti (Henry Wright), Edward, and Yakobo (Jacob). About the same time a sixth lad was baptized at Zanzibar. This was Luta (or Duta), the boy who was bound and sent away with Mukassa. He had been released, and allowed in March 1881 to accompany Mr. Pearson to the coast, and the latter had left him at Zanzibar, under the care of the Universities' Mission. On Easter Day 1882 he was baptized.

Many others were eager to follow the example of the five. A chief who had heard the word began to teach his women, and came with a boy and his *mandwa*, or priest, to Mr. O'Flaherty for further instruction. The *mandwa* threw away his priest's robe and his charms, and professed himself a believer in Jesus, the

THE SEED SPRINGING UP.

Son of God. The chief had to return to his post in the country, but he sent the *mandwa* one day with a present, and a request that Mr. O'Flaherty would visit him and his people, teach them more fully, and baptize them. This, however, was not possible at the time. Mr. O'Flaherty wrote :—

'The day the priest came here there was a large crowd of people gathered, and many priests and people of *lubare* also. When the proper time came, the *mandwa* got up like another Peter "in the midst," and stated, with the force and eloquence of an Apollos, the reasons that forced him to burn his charms, and reject the service of *lubare* for the noble service of the Son of God. All were moved, and many went away pricked to the heart.'

One most interesting case was that of a young man named Mwira, who came and begged to be allowed to remain with the missionaries while they taught him. Slower than many at learning, he made up for this by his eagerness, joy beaming in his face as he mastered each new thought. Before he went home he thus expressed himself to Mr. O'Flaherty :—

' I am like a man travelling in a mountainous country. He climbs and passes ridge after ridge with pleasure. But as he surmounts he looks before him to the heights beyond, each one loftier than those he has passed, and he becomes impatient, and wonders to himself if he will ever surmount the last. But there is one great difference. The traveller, in his desire, hastens from the summit of one ridge to descend, that he may climb another height; thence he hastens on, till he climbs the last and highest. Not so I. When I climb, I like to lie on the top and rest, and enjoy the others before. Yes, I like to rest, and drink of the fountains that gush forth as I climb. Oh the pleasure of reading and thinking upon those delightful books, and of meditating on the wonders of the Son of God becoming Man to save men from *lubare* !'

Having been some little while at home, he returned to the Mission, bringing his wife and little child. His wife he had already taught to read, but wanted more instruction for her. One morning she asked for a hoe, that she might labour in the missionaries' plantation, saying, 'I do not wish to eat your generous bread for nothing.' They were baptized under the names of Yohana (John) and Maryamu (Mary), and shortly afterwards, at their own request, married to one another after the manner of the Prayer-Book.

Two other young couples were married about the same time 'in Christ's way,' as they termed it.

Filipo Mukassa had brought his wife to be instructed. 'She was at first,' says Mr. O'Flaherty, 'a haughty savage, and would not touch our food.' She, however, joined a ladies' class which had been formed 'with much fear, and faith, and prayer,' and though at first she asked in amazement, 'Can women learn ?' she soon found herself making progress, and after some time she begged to be baptized, together with her child. 'Nothing,' writes Mr. O'Flaherty, 'has testified to the reality of the change more than the way she conducts herself. I found her one day working in the plantation with the other women. I said, "Sarah, who told you to work? I thought you were above working." She said, "I cannot wash or sew like my sisters in England; I wish I could; but I can prune and hoe, and the plantains which feed us require both. It is my duty to assist in feeding this great family."'

There were two young men in the king's household who were to be baptized with others on July 12, 1883. But two days before the time they were smitten with the plague, and were, according to custom, carried away, and left to die. They sent at once for Mr. O'Flaherty, who writes :—

'I hastened to them; the place was deserted. After a few words and a short prayer, I sent the messenger to the river for water, and poured it on the first, Makassa, in the name of the Blessed Trinity. I shall never forget the look up to heaven, and the words, among many others, to the effect that, although he was leaving an earthly palace, he was going to the palace in heaven; and turning to his friend, he said, "Jesus our Saviour is our King." His hands were clasped in mine, but in a paroxysm of burning agony he relaxed his grasp and gave up the ghost. Turning to my other friend, I found him already in the throes of death. I did not put the water on him, but I felt his name was entered in the baptismal register of heaven.'

Altogether these two years, 1882 and 1883, were a time of encouragement. There were so many to be taught that three African teachers were regularly employed—Henry Wright Duta, Filipo, and a young Swahili from Zanzibar, besides three others when necessary. 'We have,' writes Mr. O'Flaherty, 'a text-book of theology, the Lord's Prayer, Creed, Decalogue, texts of Scripture so arranged that they teach the plan of salvation, and the duties of a subject to his sovereign, and sovereign to subject, and all to Christ.' All these had been printed by Mackay—three hundred copies, besides an equal number of alphabetical spelling-sheets in Luganda—'no small work,' writes Mr. O'Flaherty, 'on a toy-press.' Morning service was conducted daily at the 'chapel' between 6 and 7 a.m., by the Rev. R. P. Ashe (who arrived in Uganda in April 1883), Henry Wright Duta reading the lessons;

besides there were two regular services on Sunday, and the chapel was full to overflowing, both with men and women.

The daughters of the king himself now became anxious to learn. His favourite daughter fell desperately ill. She was immediately surrounded by a troop of *lubare* priests and doctors, but they could do nothing for her, and at length Mr. O'Flaherty was summoned. He turned out the *lubare* priests, and his treatment was blessed to the cure of the apparently dying girl. Not long after another of the princesses visited him, saying that both she and her sister wanted his instruction, but had hitherto been afraid to come, but that what he had done for her sister had encouraged her, and she was now determined to learn the words and religion of Jesus Christ. She was baptized in September, with five other persons. The girl who had been cured of her sickness appeared to receive the truth into her heart, but later on she was carried off by small-pox. Mwira, or Yohana, the convert above mentioned, taught many others, and one of his friends, Samweli, was baptized towards the end of the year. In October 1883 twenty-one Christians of Uganda assembled together at the Lord's table to commemorate His death, for the first time. 'I wish,' writes Mr. O'Flaherty, 'you were here to see the reverence, and share in our joy.' The following year another of Mtesa's daughters was baptized; but these princesses did not prove altogether satisfactory. Another of those admitted into the Church was Sebwato, the chief above mentioned, whose *mandwa* had cast away his charms. He received the name of Nikodemo.

The small-pox, which ravaged the country in the beginning of 1884, carried off one of the first converts, Filipo Mukassa. When he died his brothers came to take away the body, but his wife Sarah supported Mr. O'Flaherty in his refusal to let it go, on the ground that the dead man was *his* brother by a more lasting tie than that of nature. Thus Filipo received the first Christian burial in Uganda. When the brothers 'saw the fine grave, and the beautiful bark-cloth, and the fine white linen (*bufta*) that were to form his shroud and winding-sheet, they consented, and they went and wound him up, and helped to carry him to the grave by lantern and lamplight. Mr. Ashe read the Creed and a short service, and they retired and came to me and said, "You have buried him a chief; we wish to be your brothers also."'

Another interesting case was that of a blacksmith, called Walukaga, with whom Mackay had made friends while engaged in one of those tasks which fell so constantly to his lot. Concerning this manual labour he once wrote :—

'I suppose that my desire to devote most, if not all of my time to studying the languages, teaching, translating, and conversing with natives, instead of working in wood, and iron, and clay, is just what every man who comes here will feel.'

But he went on, 'All intercourse with the natives helps one to acquire a knowledge of their tongue, and a complete mastery of that is necessary to be able to teach them aright. The Gospel of our glorious Lord should not be turned to ridicule by our broken utterance, when increased diligence can make us fluent speakers.'

And as he did the secular work for Christ's sake, so was it blessed to the promotion of the spiritual work. He had been requested by Mtesa, on the death of the queen-mother, Namasole, to make the coffin, or rather three coffins for her, the outer one of which was nearly as large as the enormous grave dug to receive the remains. It was in doing this work that Mackay became acquainted with Walukaga, who afterwards used to come and read with him. Walukaga was baptized with three others on September 21, and gave the missionaries much joy by his earnestness. Altogether, up to the end of 1884, there were eighty-eight baptisms, a blessed harvest from the seed sown during seven years in faith and patience.

> For wand'ring feet now treading
> With joy the heavenward way;
> For lips Thy glories spreading
> We bless Thee, Lord, to-day.
>
> S. G. S.

CHAPTER VII.

THE BEGINNING OF PERSECUTION.

'They overcame him by the blood of the Lamb, and by the word of their testimony; and they loved not their lives unto the death.'—
REV. xii. 11.

WHILE the first-fruits were being gathered in Uganda, the committee at home were not unmindful of the needs of the Mission, nor of the importance of reinforcing the brethren who held this far-off outpost. In May 1882 a party of six missionaries left England for the Nyanza. These were the Rev. James Hannington of Brighton, the Rev. R. P. Ashe, of St. John's College, Cambridge, the Revs. J. Blackburn, E. C. Gordon, and W. J. Edmonds, of Islington College, and Mr. C. Wise, an artisan. It was the deaths of Shergold Smith and O'Neill (as already mentioned) which first roused in the heart of James Hannington a desire to go out to the Victoria Nyanza, and follow up the work begun by them. In a far more literal manner than he could have foreseen, he was to follow in their footsteps, by giving, not the work of many years of life, but the far-spreading and deeply telling influence of a martyr's death, to the cause he had at heart. For some time the wish remained hidden in his own heart, or revealed only to her who was his true helpmeet in the Master's work. In November 1881 he wrote in his journal: 'It does not seem to me possible that the Church Missionary Society would accept me. I am not worthy of the honour.'

But on receiving a letter from the Honorary Secretary of the Society, Mr. Wigram, on the subject, he no longer hesitated, but at once sent in his offer of service for four years, on condition of the Society supplying his place at St. George's Chapel, Hurstpierpoint, purposing to go out, for the most part, at his own expense. The offer was gladly accepted, and he was appointed leader of the expedition.

The party reached Zanzibar on June 19, and Mr. Stokes having made all preparations for the journey to the lake, the caravan started on the 26th for the mainland, and thence by Mombasa and Mpwapwa across the plains of Ugogo, to Uyui. They took with them Henry Wright Duta, who had lately been baptized at Zanzibar, and who was attached to Hannington as his 'boy' on the march. While passing through Ugogo Hannington was attacked by violent fever, and underwent intense suffering. Nevertheless he marched on bravely, reaching Uyui, however, in a state of great prostration. Here he was seized with dysentery, and it was decided by the rest of the party that they must not attempt to take him on with them to the lake. He was accordingly left behind under charge of Mr. Copplestone, and of his nephew, Mr. Gordon; not long after acute rheumatism was added to his other sufferings, and it seemed impossible that he could live. In spite of his condition, he employed himself in drawing up a manual of information for future missionaries starting for Africa; and one day, being able to walk a short distance, he went and chose a spot for a grave, which he believed would shortly receive his earthly tabernacle.

Contrary to all expectation, the caravan which had

left him behind returned again to Uyui, the party (consisting of Stokes, Gordon, Ashe, and Wise, Messrs. Edmonds and Blackburn remaining to occupy Uyui) having met with such unreasonable demands for *hongo* on the road taken, that Mr. Stokes resolved to seek a new one. When Hannington heard the voice of the caravan leader, it seemed to inspire him with new life. 'I shall live, and not die!' he exclaimed, feeling sure the providence of God had led them back that he might accompany them. After consultation a hammock was prepared for him, and carried by porters he proceeded on with them towards the lake. The route chosen by Stokes lay west of the old one, and led them through the country of the famous Mirambo. Urambo, the capital of this potentate, where there was a station of the London Missionary Society, had been visited by Mr. Litchfield during his stay at Uyui. Mirambo himself was absent at the time, but Mr. Litchfield had been told that caravans could pass that way to the lake without paying the *hongo* extorted on other routes. Mirambo had been subsequently visited by Mr. Copplestone.

The chief of Urambo received the party favourably, and gave them a headman to conduct them to the last village in his territory, Kwa Sonda, or Msalala, on Smith Sound, the western arm of the inlet called Jordan's Nullah. Here an invitation reached them from Rwoma, chief of Buzinja, to the north of Msalala, promising them canoes in which to cross the lake. The promise, however, was not kept, and the missionaries were glad to make their escape from the country of the false chief. Hannington had now in some measure revived, and not only made the journey into Rwoma's country, but for a while had the whole burden of the expedition on his hands, Mr. Stokes having returned to Uyui, and the other missionaries being ill. He established Mr. Wise at Kagei, and then leaving him there with Mr. Gordon he returned to Msalala in terrible suffering. Finding, at length, that it was utterly impossible for him to proceed further, he took a sorrowful farewell of Mr. Ashe and Duta, turned his face from the lake, and started for the coast. 'My eyes,' writes Mr. Ashe, 'followed the tall receding figure, now indeed bowed with the intense pain and suffering he had undergone, and I wondered, as I watched him, whether he would ever accomplish the long eight hundred miles of swamp and wilderness, with its certain toils and unknown perils, which lay between him and Zanzibar.' In much pain and weakness, however, the journey was accomplished, contrary to the expectations of his porters, who more than once left him, as they thought, to die. Mr. Blackburn came from Uyui to meet him, and accompanied him to the coast, returning afterwards to his station. And so at length home was once more reached, and gradually health was given back by the Great Physician, who, as Captain of the host of the Lord, had yet work for him to do. Mr. Edmonds was compelled by ill health shortly to return home also.

Meanwhile Hannington had left behind him on the shores of the lake not only the two missionaries Gordon and Wise (Mr. Ashe having shortly after started for Uganda in some canoes of King Mtesa's), but also a silent yet substantial memorial of his journey thither. This was a mission boat to replace the Daisy. Before leaving England he had made an appeal for funds to provide the vessel, and it had been carried up country by porters, and left at Msalala until it could be put together and launched. This was done, after an infinity of toil and trouble, by Mr. Mackay.

The latter, after the arrival of Mr. Ashe in Uganda,

THE BEGINNING OF PERSECUTION. 95

left him there with Mr. O'Flaherty, and proceeded to the south of the lake, landing at Kagei, where he found Mr. Gordon and Mr. Wise. The new route taken by the last expedition to the lake rendered it advisable to remove the Mission stores from Kagei to some more suitable place; and the spot chosen was the place where Hannington had stayed, Msalala, which became for some time the head-quarters of the Mission. On examining the pieces of the vessel brought there by Hannington they were found to be in a deplorable condition. The boards had been left packed together in a tent, but in the absence of the missionaries the chief of the place had taken away the tent and thrown out the boards, and Mackay found them 'lying warping, splitting, and shrinking under a blazing sun.' Even a skilled workman like Mr. Wise thought it a hopeless task to attempt to make anything of them. But Mackay was not to be daunted. He resolved that the thing should be done. But the question was, Where should the boat be built and launched? The upper part of Smith Sound, near Msalala, is choked up with papyrus, and to go further north on the western shore would bring them into the territory of the false chief Rwoma. The pieces of the boat were accordingly carried across the sound at a place called Muleshi's Ferry, into the country of Urima, on the eastern shore (between the two arms of Jordan's Nullah). Much difficulty was now experienced in obtaining permission from the king to build the boat there. He fancied the missionaries would bewitch him with a look, and then carry off his spirit, to make a show of it to the white men at the coast! Mackay's perseverance, however, triumphed over every obstacle, and at length, on December 3, 1883, the Eleanor was launched on the shining waters over which she was to bear the messengers of peace.

In addition to her English name Mackay gave her an Arabic one, Mirembe, or 'Peace.' The name was to speak to the natives of her true mission, so widely opposed to that of the war canoes of King Mtesa and the slave-boats of the Arabs. In the Eleanor, or Mirembe, Mackay returned to Uganda; and by April 1, 1884, he had accomplished four voyages for necessary purposes in this useful little vessel.

It was but four days before Christmas when he reached the Mission premises. 'That,' writes Mr. Ashe, 'was a time of great rejoicing. A goodly band of candidates were awaiting baptism, and Mackay was back again with the beautiful boat, and a supply of stores, and best of all, our letters from England, and good news of Gordon and Wise from the south of the lake. There did not seem to be a single cloud in our sky, and the recollection of that Christmas Eve is among the brightest I can recall.'

The scene, however, soon darkened. Idle accusations were brought against the missionaries, and they found themselves under a cloud of suspicion. But still darker shadows were approaching. In spite of many ups and downs of favour, King Mtesa had been, on the whole, friendly to the work. But he had long been in a suffering condition, and at length, in October 1884, he succumbed to his disease, and throughout the country passed from lip to lip the news that the great monarch was dead. His loss could not but sadden the missionaries, who had time after time pleaded with him to accept in his heart and life the truth he knew so well with his head. Very touching is the record of Mackay's appeal to him shortly after the death of Namasole. The queen-mother had had a most costly funeral, cloth after cloth and linen in enormous quantity having been thrown into her grave, till the value had

THE EXTERIOR OF MTESA'S TOMB.
(*From a sketch by Bishop Tucker.*)

THE BEGINNING OF PERSECUTION. 99

reached about £15,000! In conversing with Mtesa on this matter Mackay took occasion to assure him how little such pomp was worth. 'Let me,' said he, 'have only an old bark cloth, and nothing more of this world's riches, and I would not exchange for all the wealth and greatness of both (the two head chiefs), because all their greatness will pass away, while their souls are lost in the darkness of belief in the *lubare*; while I know that my soul is saved by Jesus Christ the Son of God, so that I have riches that never perish.' Mtesa replied with his usual excuses about the 'two religions' put before him (the Mohammedan and the Christian).

Mackay writes: 'I left my seat, and going forward to the mat on which the *katikiro* was sitting, I knelt on it, and in the most solemn manner I said, "O Mtesa, my friend, do not always repeat that excuse. When you and I stand before God at the great day of judgment, will you reply to Almighty God that you did not know what to believe, because Masudi told you one thing and Mackay told you another? No; you have the New Testament; read there for yourself. God will judge you by that. There never was any one yet who looked for the truth there and did not find it."'

But this earnest appeal was, like many others, in vain. With all his enlightenment, knowledge, quickness of thought and perception, and the evident power which the Word had sometimes exercised over him, Mtesa died a heathen.

This sad event was the means of making manifest the wonderful influence exercised by the Gospel, even over those whose hearts are not yielded to it. A standard of right and wrong had been set up in Uganda, and even the heathen unconsciously owned it. In former times the death of the sovereign had been the signal for wholesale and indiscriminate murder, tumults, and robbery. This time it was very different. There was indeed much cause for apprehension. The news was brought to the missionaries by a friend, who whispered it at midnight under Mr. O'Flaherty's window, bidding them prepare for what might happen. The Arabs armed themselves to the teeth, and every one looked with suspicion on his neighbour. Two of the most powerful chiefs proposed attacking the Mission premises, but the *katikiro* prevented them, and gave orders that there was to be no pillaging. 'That night,' writes Mr. Ashe, 'we heard the quick beat of drums, sudden and alarming, and the sound of a great cry swept fitfully and wildly across the intervening valleys, as ever and anon a gust of wind stronger than usual brought it to our ears.' In the morning Mr. O'Flaherty and Mr. Ashe went up to the palace to offer their condolence, and present a piece of fine calico for the funeral. They found it filled with a wailing crowd, the chiefs dressed in dirty bark cloth, and weeping piteously.

Mackay was at the port on the lake, where he had had the Eleanor drawn up on the beach when the news reached him. He immediately set to work to launch her again, feeling that in case of trouble being at hand she might prove a place of refuge. The next day he returned to Natete (the Mission station), and was quickly sent for by the chiefs, to direct the native workmen in making the coffin. The whole country now went into mourning. No white or coloured clothes were seen, and the men put on girdles of withered plantain fibre, the women of leaves.

Mtesa's youngest son, Mwanga, a lad only eighteen years of age, was the one chosen to succeed him. He had often visited the missionaries, and had learned a little from them, but he is described as wayward and

THE INTERIOR OF MTESA'S TOMB.
(*From a sketch by Bishop Tucker.*)

flighty, and unable to concentrate his attention on one thing for any length of time, and, in fact, inferior every way to his father, though bearing a likeness to him in outward appearance. His brothers were spared the usual fate of princes on such occasions, and allowed to live, and the *katikiro*, contrary to custom, managed to retain office. The king changed the royal residence from Rubaga to Nabulagala.

Mwanga treated the missionaries with but scant courtesy. Shortly after his accession to the throne he requested Mackay to go to the south of the lake, and bring more white men, 'as if those beings weie to be had for the mere ordering of them.' Mackay, however, really hoped to find a reinforcement at Msalala, and, in anticipation of this, had planned to return to England in the spring. Mr. Roscoe and Mr. Yeames had, in fact, started originally for the lake. But the former remained at Mamboia, and the latter was sent to Frere Town, and, to Mackay's disappointment, there was nothing for Uganda but a cargo of goods. The voyage, in spite of this, seems to have been a time of real refreshment. It was necessary that a king's messenger, or headman, should accompany the boat, and after some attempt to force upon Mackay a man who was no friend to the Mission, the king had at length appointed one of his pages, named Mika Sematimba, a baptized Christian, to the post. Some other Christian lads went with them, and Mackay writes:—

'I had as many as nine Christians on board—a rare pleasure. In mid-lake in the midnight hours, as they sang their hymns, and joined me in prayers, I could only reflect how much sooner than I had expected a year before the small Eleanor had become in some more true way a missionary vessel.'

This little time on board the Mirembe must have

been as an oasis in the desert of toil and trial passed through by Mackay. Shut out from the sights and sounds of cruelty, from the clamour of tongues, from heathen suspicion and rage, with only the waters round him, and the open heaven above, his little Christian crew about him, he could gather fresh strength for the conflict, shortly to wax hotter and fiercer than ever. On his return to Uganda, Mwanga, being disappointed of the white men for whom he had sent, immediately resolved to supply their place by others, and sent to Ukumbi for some French priests.

Various other causes conspired to increase his ill-will towards the missionaries. The journey of Mr. Joseph Thomson through Masai Land had given rise to the report that there were white men in Busoga, a tributary state to the east of Uganda, and separated from it by the Nile. The king not unnaturally concluded that these were the men whom Mackay ought to have brought from the south end of the lake, and that they had taken another route. The Baganda had a great jealousy of any strangers coming to their country by way of Busoga, partly because they considered the approach easier than that by way of the lake, which formed a kind of natural defence to their country, and partly because of an old prophecy that Uganda was to be conquered by a people coming from the east. Once, when the easterly route was mentioned by Mackay to King Mtesa, he said, 'I know you white men want exceedingly to see what there is beyond Busoga, but I will never permit it.' Just at this time the king of half Busoga failed to come as usual with his yearly tribute of ivory. This failure was at once attributed to the presence of white men in his country, who had incited him to rebel.

The Arabs now got up a report that the missionaries

THE BEGINNING OF PERSECUTION. 105

were harbouring malefactors, a man who was arrested for some offence having been found hiding with one of the Christian converts. The anger of the king being aroused by this, the flame was fanned by Mujasi, captain of the body-guard, who was friendly with the Arabs, and had a deep-seated hatred of white men and their religion. The missionaries soon heard that Mujasi had orders to arrest all Baganda found on their premises. They at once warned the people not to visit them, and sent away some lads who had come from a distant part of the country for instruction. Some of these, however, came back in a day or two, thinking that there was in reality no danger.

In January 1885 Mr. Mackay asked leave of the king to cross the lake, wishing to take some letters to Msalala. Permission was granted, and he returned home and made preparations to leave the next day. 'Towards midnight,' he writes, 'there was a great deal of drumming, but that is so common a thing that we never heeded it. It was only too late that we knew it was Mujasi collecting an army to entrap me next morning.' Next day the party set out, Mackay's *wangwana* (coastmen) carrying the loads, and several boys who had attached themselves to the missionaries going along with them. Mackay and Ashe, who was to accompany him as far as the port, Ntebe, followed together. Every now and then they met little companies of armed men, but their suspicions were not aroused until, having nearly reached the lake, there sprang upon them from the bush several hundred men armed with guns, spears, and shields, shouting, 'Go back! go back!' They were jostled, and pushed, and forced to turn their faces the way they came, guns also being pointed at them. They walked quietly back, and hoped their boys had reached the port without molestation. But it was not so. After marching some distance, Mr. Ashe perceived his boy Lugalama being led along handcuffed. Hastening forward to undo the cords, he was driven back by the mob; but by-and-by, when the boys had disappeared, the missionaries were left to finish their march alone. They hastened at once to the *katikiro*, but could obtain no redress, and were at length violently turned out of the house and surrounded by a clamouring mob, who, however, contrary to all natural expectation, suddenly dispersed and allowed them to return to their dwelling unmolested. Thus did the providence of God watch over them. They immediately bade the lads who were staying with them to take flight; but one, Seruwanga, lingered too late, and was caught that evening by Mujasi's men. Mukassa Samweli (of whom more hereafter), and Edward Mukassa (one of the first five baptized in 1882), both servants of Mwanga, ventured to the Mission House to offer their sympathy, though unable to help. Mr. O'Flaherty went to the king next morning, but without effect. By-and-by, however, some of the boys were set free, but Seruwanga Kakumba, who had attached himself to the missionaries, and Lugalama, were led away to be put to death. Lugalama was a little Muhuma[1] boy, said to belong to one of the chief families of Karagwé, who had been captured in a raid made by the Baganda. His captor, the chief Sebwato, had treated him kindly, and on returning home sent him to the missionaries, thus practically setting him free. He now did his utmost to save him, but in vain. Another chief actually accepted a valuable present from Mr. Ashe on condition of bringing back Lugalama, when he knew the boy was no longer living.

[1] Muhuma, singular of Wahuma.

The three lads—one aged about fifteen, the youngest only eleven or twelve—were taken to the borders of a dismal swamp. Here a sort of rough scaffold was erected, and heaped with firewood. The crowd mocked and taunted the prisoners. 'Oh, you know Isa Masiya' (Jesus Christ), said Mujasi, 'you know how to read. You believe you will rise from the dead? Well, I shall burn you, and see if it be so.' The lads are said to have answered boldly and faithfully; and one report related that they had raised their voices and sung the praises of Christ in a hymn which had been translated into Luganda: 'Daily, daily, sing the praises' (*Killa Siku tunsifu*). This was afterwards contradicted. But one wonders if an African could have invented it.

The persecutors were not satisfied merely with taking the lives of these faithful lads. To death was added torture. Their arms were savagely cut off, and bleeding they were flung upon the scaffold. The youngest and tenderest had pleaded to be *only* cast into the fire, but the murderers would spare him none of the agony. There stood by one of Mujasi's men, his *musali* or guide, who related the sorrowful story afterwards. The murderer turned fiercely upon him: 'I will burn you too and your household; I know you are a follower of Isa' (Jesus). 'Yes, I am,' answered Kidza, 'and I am not ashamed of it.' But his time to suffer for Christ was not yet come.

That night, January 31, Mr. Mackay wrote in his diary: '*Our hearts breaking.*'

The fierce and cruel Mujasi now threatened to roast any one who should venture to go near the missionaries. In spite of this order, young Samweli (Mukassa) came to tell them he had been denounced to the king as a Christian, but was not afraid to die. They, however, sent him away, bidding him not to expose himself unnecessarily to danger. Sebwato, and the young admiral, Gabunga, also visited them under cover of the darkness. Samweli, who was one of the king's pages, also interceded for Sarah, the widow of Filipo Mukassa, and now the wife of Henry Wright Duta, who was in the stocks for teaching some of the princesses, and whom, with her child, Mujasi had threatened to burn. Sarah was released and sent to the missionaries; and at the same time the guard which had been set to watch their dwelling was removed. Mujasi had gone a little too far in accusing some of the chiefs, and he was sent away from the capital, while the king tried to make out that the murder of the three boys, as well as the ill treatment received by the missionaries, was purely his doing.

The death of the young martyrs was but the beginning of the 'great tribulation' through which the infant church of Uganda was to pass. But like a precious 'corn of wheat' it was to bring forth abundant fruit, not only in their own land, but among Christians at home, in stirring up the hearts of many to fresh enthusiasm and effort for the cause of Christ.

<blockquote>
And many more are crowding round to hear the Gospel word,
And many more have pledged themselves to follow Christ the Lord;
The path of suff'ring and of scorn those youthful feet have trod
Is turned into a fertile field, and beareth fruit to God.

S. G. S.
</blockquote>

CHAPTER VIII.

THE MARTYR BISHOP.

'For My Name's sake.'—JOHN xv. 21. 'For the elect's sakes.'—
2 TIM. ii. 10.

ON the removal of the guard which had been set over the Mission premises numbers at once flocked in to be taught, their eagerness in no way abated by the terror of what had taken place, and some of them were baptized. But all this was considered by the old chiefs of the country, who clung to the *lubare* worship, as *kyeju* (insolence, or 'cheek'). They began to plan rebellion against Mwanga, one of their complaints being that he was about to adopt the white man's religion (!), and alter the customs of the country. They had formed a plot to murder him at a feast in honour of the late king; but he, being informed by a relative, kept away on the occasion. The danger to the missionaries at this time was grave. Mr. Mackay writes in his journal, February 24, 1885:—

'If the rebels win we need expect little quarter, as our presence is part of the ground of complaint, and Mukwenda (one of the most powerful chiefs) it was who wished to plunder us when Mtesa died. On that occasion the *katikiro* alone is said to have prevented any one from touching us. The situation is most serious. Mirambo dead,[1] and Msalala—we know not what to

[1] They had just heard of the death of this great potentate, and feared their brethren at Msalala, whom he had favoured, might be endangered by the event.

think may have happened to it. Our boat a wreck—the only means of escape, should the rebels win. We only hope that the king, by a sharp stroke, may be able to save himself, and us with him. We commend ourselves to God in prayer, and wait for the morning.'

Next day the 'sharp stroke' was made, and the rebellion was, in the providence of God, quashed in its commencement. The chief Mukwenda was arrested and put in the stocks, and his property plundered. Seventeen other chiefs were deposed, and the king and the *katikiro* came out victorious. Several of the adherents both of the missionaries and of the French priests obtained good positions at court.

Mackay now begged permission to go to the port, and endeavour to save the Eleanor, news having been brought him that the boat was swamped. After some days' vexatious delay he obtained leave, and hastened down to the port. On emerging from the forest he 'could faintly discern among the white tops of the waves something also white, causing the waves to break higher.' The vessel was still afloat, but lying on her side, with only a few feet length of the port side above water. Hiring some canoes from the fishermen, he made for the wreck. One man dived and got hold of the anchor-chain, and the anchor was then got on board one of the canoes, and the vessel being secured by stout ropes, they pulled for shore, 'four canoes, two abreast, hauling tandem a shapeless hulk through the water.' Finally, with much difficulty and danger, the wind having changed, so that they nearly drifted on to the rocks, the boat was hauled on shore with the assistance of the friendly natives, who in their excitement jumped into the water, 'regardless of crocodiles,' to help. Thus the Mission boat was saved, to be a refuge to the missionaries in future time of need.

Feeling the precariousness of their position, and the uncertainty whether they would be able to remain in the country, the missionaries felt it desirable to make some arrangements for the carrying on of the work, in case they should be compelled to leave. Their first care was to provide for some organisation in the native Church. This was the origin of the Church Council, which was formed of men chosen by the converts themselves, the members being such as by their standing and reputation might command the respect of all. It was arranged that each convert should attach himself to some centre, presided over by an elder, so that in case of trouble there should be a rallying-point where worship might be carried on and instruction given. They further hastened to provide printed matter for those who might at any time be left without teachers. Copies of Morning and Evening Prayers, and the Baptismal Service for adults, were printed, together with Scripture texts, and some hymns in Luganda. The Gospel of St. Matthew was in process of translation, but this was far too important a work to be hurried through. 'Every sheet,' wrote Mackay, 'has to go through the hands of our best pupils again and again before they agree upon it.'

No danger, however, seemed to damp the zeal of the crowd of inquirers after Christianity, or learners already baptized. Writing in September Mr. Mackay says:—

'A great number, I may say almost all, of the pages and storekeepers, etc., about the court are pupils, either of ours or of the Papists. Again and again I have seen the various store and other houses of the court literally converted into reading-rooms. . . . Lads sitting in groups, or sprawling on the hay-covered floor, all reading; some the book of Commandments and other texts, some the Church prayers, and others the Kiswahili New Testament. They are, besides, very eager to learn to write, and at all times are scribbling on boards, or any scrap of paper they can pick up. . . . We make them pay for any paper or pens they want. Nor do we give them books, large or small, for nothing. The only things we give gratis are alphabets and many pages of syllables. But that is more in the way of advertisement. When they learn syllables they invariably buy a book. Our day-school is well attended. . . . On Sunday the numbers that come far exceed our space. But outside is large enough for all, and when the inside of our chapel is filled with classes, others find a shady corner here and there out of doors.'

Meanwhile Hannington, who since his return to England in 1883 had ever kept his eye on East Africa, had at length recovered his health sufficiently to allow of his returning thither. The Church Missionary Society Committee had long been anxious to secure for their missionaries scattered over a wide area in this part of the world episcopal counsel and supervision, and all things having been arranged with the Archbishop of Canterbury, it was felt that no more fitting man could be found than the dauntless hero who had already conducted a missionary party as far as the lake, and in whom no remembrance of sufferings endured could keep down the ardent desire to return. On June 24, 1884, James Hannington was consecrated in Lambeth Parish Church Bishop of Eastern Equatorial Africa, and shortly afterwards he started for his diocese, hoping later on to be followed by Mrs. Hannington and his youngest child, who were to reside at Mombasa. Lookers-on have wondered how this noble-hearted servant of God could start on an enterprise of such

BISHOP HANNINGTON.

peril leaving a family behind him, and have even censured him for the course he took, although they would not blame the soldier who goes forth at his country's call, undeterred by the claims of home. 'To his own master he standeth or falleth,' and he knew that the Divine Master had called him. It was not lightly that he tore himself away from his beloved ones. Writing to Mr. Fitch, Vicar of Cromer, who was parting with a son to accompany him, he says:—

'I am sure you will be blessed, ay, greatly blessed, in making the sacrifice. I am giving up three children to go out, for they cannot go with us, and nobody can tell how at times my heart bleeds. It is agony. But I can do it for Christ's sake, and I believe that He asks it of me.'

And from the vessel that bore him away he wrote to his congregation at home, unburdening his full heart in verse, almost too sacred to print. Could he only once more clasp his dear ones, he says,

> 'I would surely never leave them,
> Would never say good-bye.
> *   *   *
> But other thoughts came o'er me,
> Thoughts of the weary slave,
> Of the souls in heathen darkness
> Whom Jesus came to save.
>
> I knew that to me He whispered,
> "Leave friends in My embrace,
> And depart to tell these heathen
> Of My death and saving grace."'

All honour to her who was willing to let him go, and whose was the heaviest share of the sacrifice, if sacrifice it may be called.

After visiting the headquarters of the Mission over which he had been set, at Frere Town, as well as Taita, Chagga, and the Giriama country, he started on July 23, 1885, for Uganda. He had, not without much consideration, decided, instead of taking the usual route, to travel in a north-westerly direction from Mombasa, and strike the lake on its north-eastern shore, and reach Uganda by land. The traveller, Mr. Joseph Thomson, who had penetrated by this route nearly as far as Uganda, gave a favourable account of the climate to be passed through, the chief danger to be apprehended being from the wild tribes of the Masai met with in some parts. Hannington's main object in taking this route was the desire to open up a shorter road of communication with the missionaries in Uganda, whose perilous position, so far out of the reach of friends, lay very much on his heart. He was aware that in thus choosing a new path he was running great risks, and for this reason he resolved to take none of his own countrymen with him, and was accompanied only by Rev. William Jones, an African clergyman whom he had lately ordained at Frere Town. But of one danger, and that the worst, he was not aware, namely, Mwanga's jealousy of any white man approaching his country from the east. Of this, the cause of his cruel murder when on the very borders of the country, he was entirely ignorant, and he had started before a warning of it could reach him.

On the eve of setting forth he wrote to his wife: 'I have been very much overdone, and was as near as possible to a break-down yesterday; but to-day I am revived, and am able to send an excellent account of myself. I was delighted to think that you can trust me in His hands, who has hitherto led me by the way.'

The bishop left Rabai with his caravan on July 23. Passing the Taita country, he reached Kikumbuliu, whence, an opportunity presenting itself of forwarding despatches to the coast, he wrote his last letter, on August 11. 'The burden of my song,' he says, 'must be Praise, and the teaching of every lesson has been Trust: so comfort your heart during my absence. . . . I am quite aware that this is the easy part of the journey, and that far greater difficulties from *hongo*-demanding natives are ahead, but if this is God's time for opening up this road, we shall open it up.

* * * * * *

'And now, just leave me in the hands of the Lord, and let our watchword be, "We will trust, and not be afraid."'

On August 20, the party reached Machako's Hill, where the British East Africa Company now have a station. After crossing a grassy plain, they came to the forest highlands of Kikuyu. Here they were in terrible need of food. The Wakikuyu, having suffered ill-treatment from the Swahili traders, fled before the caravan, and all efforts to reach them and win their confidence seemed unsuccessful. Though the forest was swarming with them, it was difficult to get sight or speech of a single man. After the exercise of much tact and patience the bishop and Mr. Jones succeeded in buying food for their immediate wants, though not without incurring considerable danger from the poisoned arrows which these suspicious people, at the least alarm, would let fly. It was not till a month later, when within sight of Lake Naivasha, that they met with the Masai. They were then quickly surrounded by a crowd of the young warriors, known as El-Moran. While the older Masai are fairly friendly and peaceable, these warriors, who serve from about the age of seventeen to thirty, are the terror of the surrounding peoples. They are great cattle-raiders, and they demand heavy *hongo* from every caravan that passes. They poured into the bishop's camp, swarmed in every tent, enriched themselves with considerable *hongo*, and never left the trembling porters nor the weary bishop and his companion until darkness set in. With early morning the caravan was astir again, and soon left these troublesome and dangerous people behind.

Yet another three weeks, and they had reached the summit of the last great range of hills, and 'fair Kavirondo,' as the bishop calls it, was at their feet. They halted at the village Kwa Sundu, and here the bishop determined to leave Mr. Jones, with the greater part of the caravan, and to go forward himself with fifty men, hoping, when he reached Uganda, to send back any of the brethren who should need to return home, by way of Kavirondo, with Mr. Jones. He set out on October 12, in spite of an abscess in the foot, and walked in the next week one hundred and seventy miles. Reaching the confines of Usoga, he fell in with a disorderly troop of Baganda warriors, who seemed much excited at the sight of the white man. On the 20th he wrote: 'Through the mercy of God—and every step of the way is through His mercy—nothing happened during the night; but I fear we have arrived in a troublesome country.'

The very next day, having climbed a hill, whence to his joy he saw the Nile 'about half an hour's distance,' he was suddenly seized by some men who had followed him, dragged with extreme violence to a hut, and thrust inside the court that surrounded it. Here he was kept a close prisoner while Lubwa, the chief of the place, who was tributary to Mwanga, sent to the king to ask what was to be done with him.

In the meantime, the news of his having started for Kavirondo had reached the missionaries in Uganda, and caused them considerable uneasiness. They requested leave from the king to send the boat to Kavirondo, to meet him and bring him on. That he was going on to Busoga they had no idea. But the suspicions of Mwanga had been aroused by tidings of the advance of the Germans upon Zanzibar. The Arabs had, ever since the coming of the white men, maintained that it was the design of the foreigner to 'eat up the country. Mtesa had answered these warnings by saying: 'Let the Bazungu alone. If they mean to eat the country, surely they will not begin at the interior. When I see them begin to eat the coast, then I shall believe your words to be true.' The Bazungu had now begun at the coast, and it was not to be supposed that Mwanga would distinguish between the English and the Germans. The chiefs declared that the white men were all one, and that the missionaries were only waiting for the headmen to come, when they would begin to 'eat' the country. Said one, 'When you see running water, you may expect more to follow.' Another referred to the idea entertained by some, that if white men were killed the country would be ruined. No such result, he said, had followed the murder of the two white men in Ukerewe. And the general opinion was that the bishop must not be allowed to penetrate into their country through the 'back door' of Busoga.

Mackay brought forward a map of Europe, and endeavoured to make the king understand that the Germans and the English were distinct nations. He assured him that the chief they were expecting was a man of peace, seeking only the good of the country. It was all to no purpose. The king at length decided to send a boat with a messenger to Kavirondo to find the *askofu* (bishop), and convey him, not to Uganda, but to Msalala, until the matter had been further considered. But before the boat could reach Kavirondo the bishop was advancing into Busoga.

On October 25 a page of Mwanga's came early and reported to the missionaries that two white men[1] had arrived in Busoga; and later on another informed them that the white men had been put in the stocks. One of these, they felt sure, was the bishop. It was Sunday, and the building which served as a church was now full of people, reading in classes before the service. After conference and prayer with the Church elders, the missionaries started for the palace, some three miles off. As they entered the enclosure a lad whispered to them that messengers had already been sent to kill the white men. The king refused to see them. That night they were 'too anxious to sleep,' and were up long before dawn the next day. Again they tried to see the king, and got a note sent in to him. He sent for Père Lourdel, of the Romanist Mission, to read it to him, and the latter begged him not to bring trouble on his country by killing white men, but rather to send them back again. The same evening Mackay went up again, but could not get an interview. Three more days were passed in terrible anxiety and suspense, the king dissembling as to his intentions, and informing Lourdel that the bishop was to be sent back unhurt.

All this while Hannington was kept a prisoner, at first in a close hut without ventilation, afterwards in his own tent, which was placed within the enclosure. Here he wrote the touching entries in his diary, so wonderfully preserved in the providence of God, to tell the tale of the martyr's sufferings and faith unto the end. Racked with pain, stricken down with fever, guarded closely by soldiers, he still looked forward to release, and ultimate arrival in the country he had come so far to visit. His own cook was allowed to

[1] The bishop's cook, Pinto, was taken for a white man.

THE MARTYR BISHOP.

prepare his food, and his men were allowed to bring it him by turns. He had written a note to Mackay, which he expected would be delivered by Lubwa's messengers, but it is needless to say it never reached its destination.

On October 28 he wrote in his journal: '(Seventh day's prison.) A terrible night, first with noisy, drunken guard, and secondly with vermin, which have found out my tent, and swarm. I don't think I got one hour's sound sleep, and woke with fever fast developing. O Lord, do have mercy upon me, and release me! I am quite broken down, and brought low. Comforted by reading Psalm xxvii.

'In an hour or two fever developed rapidly. My tent was so stuffy that I was obliged to go inside the filthy hut, and soon was delirious.

'Evening; fever passed away. Word came that Mwanga had sent three soldiers, but what news they bring they will not yet let me know.

'Much comforted by Psalm xxviii.'

And on October 29, the day, as it appears, of his murder, we find the following entry:—

'Thursday—(Eighth day's prison). I can hear no news, but was held up by Psalm xxx., which came with great power. A hyena howled near me last night, smelling a sick man, but I hope it is not to have me yet.'

That morning the bishop's men, who had hitherto been allowed a certain measure of freedom, were taken, and tied two and two together. Mwanga's orders had arrived to put the whole party to death. When at length Hannington was led forth a terrible pang must have shot through his tender heart as he saw his men bound, ready to be slaughtered. But another few moments, and all sorrow was for ever to be left behind.

His last reported words, truly characteristic of his life, were a message to King Mwanga, saying he was about to die for the Baganda, and that he had purchased the road to Uganda with his life. Then he knelt down, and as the signal gun was fired the spears flashed, and the cruel work was done. The noble missionary had breathed his last. His men lay (with a few exceptions) dead or dying around him. Once more the servants of the King had been 'spitefully entreated' by those to whom they bore His message, and the martyr's blood was poured out for Africa.

And now for him who had, as far as a sinful mortal may do so, laid down his life, as a faithful shepherd, for the wandering sheep entrusted to his care, the 'crown of glory that fadeth not away,' and, better still, the immediate presence of the Master whom he loved, and in whose footsteps he had sought to follow.

That day, October 29, Mackay wrote in his journal:—

'No news all day. . . . A few of our people about. They take a gloomy view of the situation, and do not believe that the last messengers were sent to cancel the order (for the white men's death), but to confirm it. The king pretended that he had forwarded a letter from Mackay to the bishop, together with orders to send him back. He kept up this dissimulation even after the murder had been committed.

But the next day the news arrived. Mackay writes, on October 30:—

'After dark Ismail came to tell us that messengers had returned from Busoga with the tidings that the white men had been killed, and all their porters. . . .

'Oh night of sorrow! What an unheard-of deed of blood!'

Yet so contradictory were the reports, that for some

days more hope alternated with fear. Not till November 5 did the news seem confirmed with certainty, and Mackay wrote :—

'We have no hope now for the bishop. The worst seems over. Our dear brethren[1] are happy. We remain in the midst of death. Lord, Thy will be done!'

And so the long-tried missionaries, who had looked forward to welcoming helpers and friends in the work, were left to face the threatening storm alone.

But we must go back to Mr. Jones, left with his band of one hundred and fifty men at Kwa Sundu. Day after day he waited, with increasing anxiety, for news from his chief. At length, nearly a month after the parting, four of the survivors arrived with the terrible news. As they could not give a satisfactory account of how they managed to escape, Mr. Jones refused to believe their report, and suspected them of having deserted from their leader. Another month he waited at Kwa Sundu; but at length, finding the sad news confirmed, he sorrowfully turned with his caravan once more towards the coast. On February 4 the party limped into Rabai, worn, weary, ragged, in their van the *kilongozi*, or guide, bearing a blue flag (the African colour of mourning), with the word 'Ichabod' in white letters upon it; in their rear the 'battered white helmet' of the sorrowing leader.

In the safe arrival of the diminished caravan, whose return journey had been made in sorrow and want, and who had had to encounter the dangers and privations of the way without the presence which had so encouraged and animated them when they went forth, we may trace the answer to the prayers of Hannington for his 'poor men.' They had been much on his heart when

---
[1] Supposing there were two white men.

starting, and he had rested himself on the promise which came to him as a direct message of God concerning them : 'The Lord preserveth the strangers.'

It was on January 1, 1886, that the first rumour of the sad event reached England. On Sunday evening, February 7, came the telegram from Frere Town confirming it, which called forth a burst of mourning from all the friends of Missions. But greater perhaps than this was the universal interest and sympathy which the recital of the martyr bishop's sufferings and death called forth. By his life he had spoken loudly. By his death a hundredfold had been added to his testimony—a testimony to that constraining love and sustaining grace which enables a man gladly and patiently to lay down his all at the call, and for the sake of his Heavenly Master.

'Soldier, rise—the war is done;
  Lo, the hosts of hell are flying;
'Twas thy Lord the battle won;
  Jesus vanquished them by dying:
Pass the stream—before thee lies
  All the conquered land of glory;
Hark what songs of rapture rise,
  These proclaim the victor's story—
    Soldier, lay thy weapons down,
    Quit the sword and take the crown ;
Triumph ! all thy foes are banished,
Death is slain, and earth has vanished.'

Anon.

CHAPTER IX.

THE GREAT PERSECUTION.

'A burning fiery furnace.'—DAN. iii. 6.

THE year 1885 closed for the missionaries in Uganda, as it had begun, in clouds and darkness, interspersed with gleams of brightness from the heaven beyond. The murder of their bishop meant something more than deep sorrow for them. It meant continued loneliness and isolation, and graver danger than ever. The prestige which seemed to surround the person of a white man had been broken through. One such, and that one a chief, had fallen at the tyrant's command. What was there to prevent his taking the lives of the others? At the same time Mwanga was conscious that he had committed a deed likely to rouse the anger of the bishop's countrymen, and his fears lest vengeance should reach him rendered him even more hard and cruel. Again, he was enraged at the white men getting information about the things he wished to hide from them. It was the case of Benhadad, king of Syria, over again: 'Will ye not show me which of us is for the king of Israel?'[1] 'Mwanga complained,' writes Mackay, 'that we know all his secrets from his own pages.' Certain it is that these lads knew the danger they incurred in bringing news to the mission house,

[1] 2 Kings vi. 11.

and yet did not shrink from it. 'The devotion and courage of these young Christians,' writes Mackay, 'are wonderful.'

Various warnings reached the missionaries of the king's feelings towards them. One of the princesses sent word that if ever they needed to propitiate Mwanga it was now, since when he killed any one, the friends of the dead man were regarded as enemies, unless they made the king a present to show that this was not the case. A present was accordingly sent, both to him and to the *katikiro*. It appeared, however, to produce at first a contrary effect to the one intended, the king being angry that they should be sufficiently informed as to the situation to think it necessary to propitiate him. The next day came a peremptory command for Mackay to go to the palace. He knelt with Mr. Ashe to pray before facing the tyrant. 'Very humble,' writes Mr. Ashe, 'very weak, very childlike he was on his knees before God; very bold, very strong, very manly afterwards, as he bore for nearly three hours the browbeating and bullying of Mwanga and his chiefs.' The king set himself, first by threats and then by cajolings, to find out who had told them about the bishop's murder—if they would only reveal this they should be great favourites. Their silence incensed him greatly, and he cried, 'What if I kill you? What could Queeni (the Queen) do? What could she or all Europe do?' Père Lourdel, who was present, attempting to put in a word, was at once extinguished with, 'If I killed them, should I spare you?' After more abuse Mwanga suddenly called to an attendant saying, 'Take these men, and give them two cows to quiet their minds' (!), and the court was dismissed. Thus were they again, in the good providence of God, saved from the mouth of the lion.

Orders were, however, issued forbidding any one to go near their premises, on pain of arrest and death to themselves. In spite of this, a message was brought them at midnight from the young admiral, Gabunga, who for some time had read with the missionaries and attended their services, asking for baptism. 'So it is, and will ever be,' writes Mackay : 'some will press into the kingdom in times of the greatest trial.'

Now appeared the wisdom of having appointed Church 'elders,' who could assemble at their own houses a few Christians and others desirous of being taught, with less danger than if they had attempted to visit the missionaries. Gabunga and five others were baptized, after proper examination, at the house of the blacksmith before mentioned, Walukaga Nua. The house of this man, Mr. Ashe writes, was 'quite a sanctuary in times of trouble.' Sembera Mackay and others also collected around them little congregations for reading and prayer.

It was at this juncture, when, humanly speaking, everything around looked dark and black, that the first sheet of St. Matthew's Gospel in Luganda made its appearance, three hundred and fifty copies being printed off on November 13, 1885. Only two days later another martyrdom took place. Balikudembe Mukasa, the king's head page, had been for some time a reader with the missionaries. Then the Romish priests got hold of him, and persuaded him to join them. He continued, however, a friend to his first teachers, and showed sympathy with them in the time of trial. Balikudembe dared to tell his royal master that it was wrong to have put Bishop Hannington to death, as white men were the benefactors of the country. 'See,' said the king, 'this fellow wants to insult me.' He was sentenced to be burnt alive, and the *katikiro* gave orders for this to be done at once, before the king had time to change his mind (as he afterwards did). The executioner, who was a friend of the brave lad, killed him before committing his body to the flames. It appears that Balikudembe had often spoken to the king, and had exhorted him to put away his charms. 'Brave lad,' writes Mackay, 'thou hast witnessed faithfully for thy Master here below. Enter into the joy of thy Lord.' Other Christians were also arrested, one of them the sub-chief Sebwato (Nikodemo), besides several pages who had gone to see Balikudembe after his arrest.

These were afterwards set free, and a short time of comparative peace followed. Mackay and Ashe continued to work hard at printing, getting assistance in translation from their converts. The former writes, on December 8:—

'The whole of the Sermon on the Mount is now in type. Every proof sheet we distribute several copies of among our people, and have their corrections and emendations before going to press. They take a deep interest in the work in this way, and are proud to have *their own* Gospel.'

Later on, many of the bishop's effects having been brought from Busoga by Mwanga's agents, a diary of his journey from the coast to Kwa Sundu was given to the missionaries by a Christian lad, who purchased it of the king's gatekeeper.

By the close of the year Mr. O'Flaherty had obtained permission to leave, and Mackay and Ashe were left alone. The former died on his way home, in the Red Sea.

In February 1886 Mwanga's palace was burned to the ground, the fire originating in his gunpowder store. He fled in the greatest terror, and made a temporary capital for himself on the creek. After this, Mr. Ashe writes, 'Mwanga was gradually becoming disagreeable again. He had said after the fire that the white men had bewitched him, and would be the death of him some day.' He ordered Mackay to bring his boat to a certain spot on the shore, and then instructed the executioner to take men and go to meet him, and to cut off his head. Mackay was, however, warned in time, and kept away from the place.

A darker time now drew on. On Easter Sunday, 1886, there was a report that the Christians were to be seized. This prevented their assembling together in any large numbers; nevertheless, twenty-five people altogether partook of the Lord's Supper that day, some of them for the last time.

In May the king's anger was aroused by one of the princesses flinging away her charms and burning her ancestral relics. It was still further excited by the refusal of one of his pages, baptized by the name of Matia, to commit a shameful sin. The boy was severely beaten, and put in the stocks, and the king began to let loose his fury against the Christian 'readers.' Two other boys were called into his presence. Mwanga attacked one of them with his spear, and then sent him to execution. Turning to the other, Kagwa Apollo, he cried, 'Are you a reader?' The lad replied in the affirmative. 'Then,' shouted the king, 'I'll teach you to read,' and seizing his spear he broke the handle on the boy's back, and gashed him about the head with the blade, only ceasing when passion had exhausted him. Wonderful to say, the boy recovered.

This savagery was but the beginning of a frightful outbreak of persecution. The following morning Mr. Ashe was sitting in the verandah behind the mission house, surrounded by his pupils. They had just been singing a hymn :—

> 'All the people bow before Thee
> Thou, the Ruler of the heavens

when Mr. Mackay entered, with the news that the king had given orders to seize all Christians. Quickly the pupils were hurried away through a hole in the back fence, just in time to escape the king's officer, who came to search for them. Mwanga now let loose his fury against all who were either known or suspected to be 'readers.' Chiefs were bidden to give up any of their people who answered to this description. Everywhere the officers were busy. The picture given in Heb. xi. of sufferers for the faith seems prophetic of what happened so long after in a country so long unheard of. They 'were tortured, not accepting deliverance, that they might obtain a better resurrection. They were . . . slain with the sword; they wandered about in sheepskins and goatskins, being destitute, afflicted, tormented (of whom the world was not worthy); they wandered in deserts and in mountains, and in dens and caves of the earth.'

Some of the Christians refused to flee into hiding, lest they might give their enemies any ground for the oft-repeated accusation of them as disloyal and seditious. One of these was Walukaga Nua, the blacksmith. While his wife escaped he quietly awaited the executioners, made no resistance when seized, and while in captivity appealed to his jailers to embrace the service of the Master for whom he was ready to suffer.

Another was Munyaga Roberto, the man who had recovered Bishop Hannington's Bible, and who had insisted on himself paying part of the price for it. He was engaged in prayer with some boys when the

THE GREAT PERSECUTION. 131

executioners arrived at his house. Springing up, all but one of these made their escape through the reed wall. Munyaga remained quiet. There was a gun leaning against his door, and seeing this the executioners paused. But the noble martyr bade them fear nothing, as he did not intend to use the gun, and only requested leave to put on his *kansu* (white robe) before they led him away. Yet another, Alexandro, went boldly up to the court, and there confessed himself a Christian.

Of what was passing the missionaries had no certain news. They only heard rumours of horrible tortures and death suffered by their converts. There came also a report that the Mission premises were to be sacked. Eight little boys residing with them were at once sent away for safety. 'We most earnestly ask,' writes Mackay, 'that in case of our deaths these boys may be sought out and recovered.' They then asked the French priests to join with them in taking steps to try and procure the release of the Christians who were in durance. The request was refused; the Frenchmen fearing that such combined action might exasperate the king yet further. On May 29 Mr. Mackay went himself to see Mwanga at his temporary palace by the lake. He reminded the latter of a promise made to him that he should have whatever he might wish for in payment of some work done for the king. 'What do you want?' asked Mwanga. 'I want,' said Mackay, 'the lives of the people you have seized.' The king promised to grant his request; but he had no intention of keeping his word. Some had actually already perished. A few days later the rest were brought out for death. The scaffold was ready, the flames were kindled around them, and thirty-two brave, devoted martyr spirits, having witnessed faithfully for their Master here below, went up to hear His 'Well done!' and enjoy His immediate presence.

Among those who perished were the men already mentioned. Munyaga was said to have been put to death with exceptional cruelty, one limb after another being cut off and flung into the fire before the final committal to the flames. Another was Kidza, or Fredi Wigram, who as *musali* (guide) to the persecutor Mujasi had witnessed the death of the first three boy-martyrs, and had on that occasion boldly confessed himself to be a Christian. His master, Mujasi, had actually warned him to flee, being probably unwilling to lose a faithful and useful servant, but Kidza refused to do so. Mr. Ashe speaks of him as 'gentle, loving, and brave, one of God's noblest martyrs,' and says: 'When I visited the scene of our children's murder it was he who led me to the place. When we reached it he knelt with me and poured out his heart to God, that He would bring His salvation to those in darkness.' Truly that prayer was heard, though he and many others had first to pass through torture and fire. Walukaga, Munyaga, and Kidza were members of the Church Council.

The demeanour of the martyrs made a great impression on the head executioner. He came and reported to the king that he had never killed men who showed such fortitude and endurance, and that they had prayed aloud to God in the fire—prayed, no doubt, like the Master of whose cup they drank—for their murderers, and for their country. But Mwanga only replied, amid the merriment of the court, that 'God had not rescued them from his power.'

All these details were reported to the missionaries by converts who had eluded the king's officers, and who sought their dwelling under cover of the night.

SCENE OF THE FIRST BOY MARTYR'S DEATH.

THE GREAT PERSECUTION.

One of their first visitors at this time of trial was an old chief who had been deposed by the king, called Isaya.[1] Some of his own lads (retainers) were under sentence of death, and after relating the death of the martyrs, he burst into tears and a terrible wail : 'They are going to kill my children ! my children !' But by the merciful providence of God he was spared this trial, and his people were left unmolested. Another visitor was a little boy called Kiwobe, who had been instructed by Munyaga Roberto. Nothing intimidated by the shocking death of his teacher, he came to Mr. Ashe with the request :—

'My friend, I wish to be baptized.'

'Do you know what you are asking ?' was the reply.

'I know, my friend.'

'But you know if you say you are a Christian they will kill you.'

'I know, my friend.'

'But suppose people asked you if you were a reader, could you tell a lie, and deny it, and say No ?'

'I shall confess, my friend.'

He was baptized by the name of Samuel.

Two other visitors who brought news were anxious to know if believers yet unbaptized (of whom some must have perished) were sure of salvation. They were of course told that where the omission of baptism did not arise from disobedience to our Lord's command, it was well with them. To these two the missionaries gave some papers and a printed letter to circulate among the Christians in hiding. The letter was as follows :—

'PEOPLE OF JESUS WHO ARE IN BUGANDA.

'OUR FRIENDS,—We, your friends and teachers, write to you to send you words of cheer and comfort,

[1] See page 74.

which we have taken from the Epistle of Peter the Apostle of Christ. In days of old Christians were hated, were hunted, were driven out, and were persecuted for Jesus' sake; and thus it is to-day.

'Our beloved brethren, do not deny our Lord Jesus, and He will not deny you on that great day when He shall come with glory. Remember the words of our Saviour, how He told His disciples not to fear men, who are only able to kill the body; but He bid them to fear God, who is able to destroy the body together with the soul in the fire of Gehenna.

'Do not cease to pray exceedingly, and to pray for our brethren who are in affliction, and for those who do not know God. May God give you His Spirit and His blessing! May He deliver you out of all your afflictions! May He give you entrance to eternal life through Jesus Christ our Saviour!

'Farewell. We are the white men; we are your brethren indeed who have written to you.'

On the other side of the page was printed 1 Peter iv. 12-19.

'What anguish of soul we have experienced,' writes Mr. Mackay, 'no words can express. This dreadful massacre has not, however, come unexpectedly. Ever since the king came to the throne things have tended that way. Again and again we have felt ourselves on the verge of it.' 'But,' writes Mr. Ashe, 'terrible as has been the slaughter, some of the very best of our people having been burnt, yet so far we have the deepest cause for thankfulness that a great house full of pages who are our converts have up to the present been spared. A similar house, containing the converts of the French priests, was taken, and some thirty of the boys were burned alive. The reason that our lads were spared is that the head storekeeper, a powerful chief, interceded for them. They are most useful to the king, which perhaps, too, has had some influence in saving their lives.'

As night after night passed, and the rest of the missionaries was broken in upon by some fresh visitor, great was their joy when well-known faces turned up which they had hardly expected to see again. Some came for baptism, men, boys, and even women; one of these a princess named Nahuita. One young chief had been a pupil of one of the martyrs named Dan.

In the hush of night, by the dim lamplight, the sacred ordinance was administered, and the converts promised 'to confess Christ crucified, and manfully to fight under His banner against sin, the world, and the devil, and to continue His faithful soldiers and servants unto their lives' end.'

Henry Wright Duta and Samweli Mukassa were under sentence of death as prominent friends of the Mission. The former was in hiding, but the latter was absent on the king's business. Samweli was a thoroughly upright, earnest Christian, and had taught his mother and grandmother, so that they had thrown away their charms, learned to read, and received baptism. Though only eighteen years of age, he had been elected a member of the Church Council by an almost unanimous vote. One morning at 3 A.M. Samweli, with two or three others, made his appearance. He was in great perplexity, and had come to the missionaries to help him. He had been commissioned by the king to collect the tribute of cowrie shells in Busongora. On his way back to the capital he heard of the persecution which had broken out, and found that he himself was to be put to death. His companions urged him to fly; but there was the tribute he had collected—what was he to do with that? If he failed to deliver it, the name of a Christian might be coupled with that of a dishonest servant. 'Tell me what you think,' said Mr. Ashe. 'My friend,' was the reply of Samweli, 'I cannot leave the things of the *kabaka* (king).' They knelt down together and prayed, and it was then arranged that Samweli should start early with his carriers, so as to leave the loads of shells with the storekeeper before the executioners were abroad. It was uncertain whether the men would agree to this haste, uncertain whether the tribute-gatherer would have time to escape after giving up his charge; but he did not hesitate. The way to the storekeeper's enclosure was taken. On reaching the place, Samweli walked boldly in and deposited his loads, came out again and walked coolly on till out of sight, and then sped off with all possible celerity, rejoicing the missionaries' hearts by appearing at their door a few nights later to report himself safe, as well as to ask questions about the saints who came out of their graves after the resurrection, and of the meaning of our Lord's words about St. John ('If I will that he tarry till I come,' John xx. 22).

It was about this time, on June 19, that Mackay obtained from the king's storekeeper the last diary of Bishop Hannington, which he afterwards sent to England. We can imagine the two missionaries, in the midst of their own trials, shedding tears over the account of the martyr's last days, spent so near to them, while he was yet, alas! beyond their reach.

While the persecution was at its height, Dr. Junker, the Russian traveller, arrived at the mission house. He had contrived to send a letter to Mr. Mackay, to announce his desire to come to Uganda on his way to the coast. He was then at Kabarega's capital in Bunyoro, and probably in some danger. Mr. Mackay had exerted himself in his behalf, so that he was conducted safely to Buganda. He brought a fearful account of what he had seen on reaching the country, the mutilated bodies of those slain in the persecution lying by the wayside. Of these only a few were baptized persons. The chiefs had all been ordered to give up the 'readers' among their followers, and a wholesale butchery had followed. Even on the road to the king's enclosure Mr. Ashe had seen the ghastly sight of a dissevered head and limbs lying on the pathway. Through Mr. Mackay's influence Dr. Junker, after a brief stay, was allowed to leave Uganda in the Eleanor.

When he was well on his way, the missionaries proceeded to ask leave of the king to quit the country, which they had delayed doing, for fear of involving him in their troubles. Their object in this demand was not the desire to escape from the scene of trials, but the persuasion that it was the strongest protest they could make against the horrible cruelties committed. But Mwanga was not anxious to lose them. His first answer was a point-blank refusal, expressed in his usual insulting manner. Mr. Mackay, however, returned to the attack. Taking with him a present, he obtained a further interview with Mwanga, and told him he intended to go. 'I will never consent to that,' replied Mwanga. Finally he agreed to Mr. Ashe's departure ; and on August 25, 1886, the latter took his leave, and hastened home to England, to tell yet more vividly than could be done by writings, the story of the sufferings, faith, and endurance of the Buganda martyrs.

But the sad, yet joyful tale had already evoked the profoundest sympathy, not only in England, but in far-off Mission fields. The Christians of Tinnevelly resolved to devote their Christmas offertories to the relief of their suffering brethren in Africa, and the sum of £80 was collected and sent to England for the purpose, with a letter full of sympathy, signed by the native pastor of Palamcotta. This brotherly offering came in usefully for the succour of the exiled Christians from time to time, especially after the revolution of 1888.

> 'High honour theirs to prove,
>   Still stands redemption's sign,
> Not lost the type of love,
>   Nor quenched the martyr line.'
>   REV. G. ENSOR (*Gleaner*, May 1878).

CHAPTER X.

FRESH LABOURERS AND FRESH SORROWS.

'Always bearing about in the body the dying of the Lord Jesus.'—
2 COR. iv. 10.

FOR about another year Mr. Mackay continued alone in Uganda, constant in work, and constant in danger. In January 1887 he wrote to Mr. Ashe: 'For a couple of months after you left I was having a regular houseful of strangers every evening. The tin of petroleum arrived just in time, as by it I could make a respectable light, and the library became a night-school. Late, late, often very late, we wound up, and I was often more than exhausted—reading, teaching, drugging, etc. By day I got, off and on, some translation done.'

Then an order went out from the king, on account of some robberies which had been committed, to arrest all found on the roads after dark, so that those in hiding could not venture near the mission house. Others, however, came by day, and often remained there all night until the morning.

On March 6 he wrote again: 'By the grace of our loving Lord I am still in the body. But were it not for the overruling hand of God, I fear there would be nothing to report but tears and groans, if there were even one left to report at all. Since receiving the mail —some six months' letters all at once—I have had the consciousness strongly forced upon me that our very existence here is mightily due to the prayers of you and all the children of God in Europe. We have had a period of respite, but once more the enemy seems to be let loose, and trouble is more than in the air. Less than a month ago we had another scare on a Sunday morning, and I had to dismiss our little congregation suddenly. The king had given out that he intended making another onslaught on the Christians; but happily he has been hitherto prevented from his bloodthirsty design. One or two of those in hiding had ventured to come to light, and nothing was done to them. Then another one or two prisoners for the faith were liberated, and intimation was made that all others in hiding might return. One ventured. He had been a page, and was at once sent by the king to the *katikiro*, but has been no more seen.'

There was evidence that this boy had been secretly murdered. Among the Christians who had all along been left unmolested, owing to their usefulness to the king, was Edward Hutchinson, one of the first five baptized converts. He was one of the most powerful of the sub-chiefs, and had built the king a new palace when the former one was destroyed by fire. He was, however, unpopular in the country, and was at length shot by an enemy. Mika Sematimba, once a page, now a sub-chief and officer in the king's body-guard, was sent to cut canes for rebuilding the king's fences. On the way his boy, who carried a bundle of things for him, was robbed. In the bundle were found some books, among them the New Testament in Kiswahili. Mika fled away, and executioners were sent after him in all directions, but happily without result.

The fickle king took up Mohammedanism again for a short time, and ordered all his pages to read the

Koran. Many of them refusing, he complained that they compelled him to be ever killing them, so that people would call him a madman! He more than once announced his intention to 'kill very many.' However, Namasole, the queen-mother, though a heathen, sent to warn him against putting to death those who were the chief strength of his country.

In spite of teaching, weaving, carpentering, printing, etc., Mr. Mackay continued to press on with the work of translation, and in March 1887 he had the whole of St. Matthew's Gospel in Luganda MS. Every page had been criticised and revised by his most advanced pupils, so as to make it as faithful a rendering of the Word of God in the tongue of Uganda as was possible. The edict for catching people on the roads at night 'gradually became more and more a dead letter,' and pupils returned in numbers. In May he wrote: 'Of late we have been reading in the evenings several of the most difficult epistles right through. To-night we had the seventh, eighth, and ninth chapters of Romans, with a good class. The argument they seem quite to comprehend. Where is Thomson, with his feeble scheme of Islam for Africa? or Reichard, with his charge of extreme poverty of mental power in the negro?'

Meanwhile, in spite of loneliness, danger, and sadness, which came over him at times, till he found himself 'shedding tears like a child,' Mr. Mackay writes:—

'I am exceedingly thankful that O'Flaherty, Junker and Ashe have all been permitted to escape in peace, and are safe from the clutches of this boy-tyrant. He pretends that his reason for not allowing me to go is his affection for me.' But, writing of Mwanga, he goes on: 'Unless the Lord has mercy on him, he will come to grief some day. He is at present exasperating his chiefs and people by his high-handedness with them.' These words were prophetic. But the time was near when the missionary was to bid adieu to the man who feared, hated, valued, and tormented him. On July 12 he writes:—

'Since the last entry in my note-book I have had a month of trouble and anxiety. The existence of the Mission has been wavering in the balance, and is even yet undecided. Our enemies (the Arabs) have tried their very utmost to prevail.' The object of the Arabs was either to kill or to get rid of one who had, from the beginning, been the firm opposer of their wicked deeds, and the king lent but a too ready ear to them. A letter which arrived for Mwanga from the English Consul at Zanzibar was, as once on a former occasion, mistranslated by the Arabs. They moreover endeavoured to inflame the king's anger against Mackay, by representing his object as a political one, and they further dilated upon Stanley's expedition in search of Emin Pasha, and magnified the force he had with him. After much disputing, and questioning, and badgering, it was decided that Mackay should leave the country, and that he should send on another English missionary to take his place. This spoiled the plan of the Arabs, who had hoped to plunder the station after his departure.

Carefully all stores were put away and locked up. The Church Council was then summoned, and provision made for the relief of the Christians in distress through flight or imprisonment. This was done by Mr. Mackay selling a tusk of ivory, presented by Emin Pasha to the Mission, in acknowledgment of his services, so as to advance the money, charging it to the Tinnevelly fund. Every copy of St. Matthew in Luganda, to the number of one hundred and sixty, was bought up by the converts, as well as all the syllable sheets recently printed, and night and day the mission house was thronged with people regretting his departure.

The last plot of the Arab Suleiman, Mackay's archenemy, was to get himself appointed as *mubaka*, or messenger, to take him across the lake; but Mackay being warned, requested Mwanga to appoint one of his own people. Finally, on July 21, he locked up the Mission premises, left the keys with the French priests, and, worn with worry, work, and farewells, started for the port, where he had to patch and repair the Eleanor before starting on his voyage. He reached the south end of the lake on August 1.

Before proceeding further we must go back, and take a hasty glance at the stations founded by the early missionaries to the lake, and which might be classed as belonging to the Victoria Nyanza Mission. These were Uyui, in Unyamwezi, and Msalala. Uyui was visited by Lieutenant Smith in 1876, and afterwards by Mr. Mackay. It was first occupied by Mr. Copplestone in 1879. When the latter's health forced him to return to England, his place was taken by Messrs. Edmonds and Blackburn, who went out with Hannington in 1882. But the former was soon obliged to follow his predecessor home, being disabled by sunstroke.[1] Progress at Uyui was slow, as, although the people were friendly, they manifested no interest at all in spiritual things. They would listen to Mr. Blackburn as he told them the story of the cross, but never even ask a question. Gradually, however, some were led to attend the services, and boys were brought under regular instruction. The first converts were baptized on July 12, 1885, and consisted of an old and faithful servant of the missionaries, called Saburi, and six boys.

[1] He afterwards went out to Japan, but died there in 1889.

In May 1875 Mr. Douglas Hooper, of Trinity Hall and Ridley Hall, Cambridge, who had been most active in stirring up and fostering a missionary spirit in that university, sailed for East Africa. He went at his own charges, taking with him Mr. S. G. Burr, who had been a gardener, and a member of the Men's Night School at Mildmay. They started for Uganda by the old route; but on reaching Mamboia, Mr. Burr, who had been suffering from fever and dysentery, became worse, and passed away on September 9, 1885, making the seventh missionary who had laid down his life for Uganda (Bishop Hannington was the eighth). His last intelligible words were, 'Peace, perfect peace,' and, 'You know the commandment, "Do all to the glory."'

Mr. Hooper went on to Msalala, and was intending to proceed to Uganda, when news arrived of Hannington's murder, and the uncertain state of matters at Mtesa's capital, which made it unadvisable for any fresh missionary to proceed there. In April 1886 he removed to Uyui, and took Mr. Blackburn's place when the latter was obliged to return home to recruit. He did not meet with much encouragement, save among the boys whom he had gathered about him, and in the following year the station had to be given up.

Msalala, as before related, was first occupied by Hannington and his party in 1883, when the Mission stores were removed thither from Kagei. Here the Rev. E. C. Gordon remained with Mr. Wise, while Mr. Ashe went on to Uganda. He found the attitude of the people very unlike that of which he had heard in Uganda. 'We have no eager seekers,' he writes, 'after knowledge, no thirst for book-lore, which can be turned to the best advantage by teaching the thirsty learners to read, and putting the Book of books into

BISHOP HENRY PERROTT PARKER.
(*By permission of Messrs. Elliott & Fry.*)

their hands. Here we have a hunger and thirst, a real demand for cloth. They say: "We will work for cloth at almost any price or rate you like to give." The people here are distinguished by a remarkable taste for music.' Mr. Gordon wrote that he quite enjoyed their occasional musical performances. He endeavoured to turn this taste to good account by teaching the boys hymns in Kiswahili. But in February 1886 the village nearest the Mission station was attacked by hostile chiefs in the neighbourhood, and its chief, Chasama, made prisoner. From that time the victors continued to harass the Mission, demanding perpetual presents in the most insolent manner. This eventually led to the giving up of Msalala as a station.

The abandonment of Uyui and Msalala took place during the brief episcopate of Bishop Parker. The second Bishop of Eastern Equatorial Africa was a graduate of Trinity College, Cambridge, and had filled for six years the post of Corresponding Secretary of the Church Missionary Society in Calcutta, first as joint worker with Mr. Welland, then in a precarious state of health, and after his death as sole Secretary. In 1885 he was in England, and spoke at the Annual Meeting of the Society; but towards the close of the year he returned to India, to take up, at his own earnest desire, direct evangelistic work among the Gonds of the Central Provinces. It seemed to the committee that no fitter man than the Rev. Henry Perrott Parker could be found to carry on the work, begun by Hannington, of superintending and caring for the different missions and missionaries in East and Central Africa. He was loth to leave the people among whom he had begun to labour, but on the promise being made that another man should be sent in his place he yielded to the request of the committee, and returned to England. He took leave of the committee at the Valedictory Dismissal in September 1886, and was consecrated shortly after at St. James's, Paddington.

'Always bearing about in the body the dying of the Lord Jesus, that the life also of Jesus might be made manifest in our body,'[1] was the text from which the Rev. H. C. G. Moule preached on the occasion. 'In the body, in our body; that is to say, in our action and intercourse, in our experiences of doing and suffering, in those countless contacts with our surroundings which constitute the reality of common life, life among men, and which are all affected through the organs and faculties of the body. In the body, —that is to say, in eyes that watch, in lips that speak, in hands that work, whether on the tent-cloth or the manuscript, in feet, that pace the city or the desert, in brain used and worn by the vivid mind; in the body given up for work, given up for suffering, along the path of life and labour for the Lord,—in this we always carry about His dying.' What a true picture do the words give of a missionary's life, and how thoroughly were they illustrated in the short career of him at whose consecration they were spoken!

Bishop Parker started for his diocese on November 3. At Lamoo he met Mr. Ashe, then on his way to England, and heard with concern of the state of Mr. Mackay's health and his need of assistance. A warm reception awaited him at Frere Town, and before the year closed he had visited Rabai and Kisulutini, and the Giriama country, as well as Zanzibar. In the beginning of 1887 he visited the Shimba country, Taita, and Chagga, and in June he set off for the lake, travelling across country from Rabai to Mamboia, and thence by the old route, accompanied by Mr. Blackburn,

[1] 2 Cor. iv. 10.

whose health was now restored. They reached Uyui in September, and after consulting with Mr. Hooper the bishop came to the conclusion that the station must be abandoned. The example of the chief at Msalala had been followed by the chief at Uyui. His covetousness was aroused by the fact of large stores for the supply of other stations being deposited here, and his demands for *hongo* were constantly increasing, while he once threatened to shoot Mr. Hooper if they were not complied with. A more friendly chief in the neighbourhood, Mtinginya, promised to take care of any goods that might be deposited with him, and accordingly, the bishop having started for the lake, Mr. Hooper began the packing and removing. While this was going on the chief of Uyui arrived himself with some of his men, in a great fury. After some time, however, he calmed down in a wonderful way, and left in a friendly manner. 'Ah, Saburi,' said Mr. Hooper to his faithful servant, 'we have seen the working of God this afternoon.' 'Truly, God is wonderful,' replied the latter. And Mr. Hooper writes: 'Never did I feel more conscious that all was of the Lord. . . . He (the chief) came up very, very angry, and I did not give in one iota. . . . The outcome was that he withdrew all he said the day before about shooting any *wangwana* (coastmen, porters), begging his 'very dear friends' to stay on. A few days later he gave permission for all the goods to be removed, and Mr. Hooper proceeded with them to Kwa Mtinginya, in Usonga, the chief left behind expressing a hope that he would soon return. At Kwa Mtinginya he found Mr. Ashe, who after spending six months in England had returned to the field, bringing with him his friend the Rev. R. H. Walker; a lay missionary, Mr. D. Deekes, had followed them there.

In the meantime Msalala had also been abandoned. On Mr. Mackay's arrival there from Uganda, Mr. Gordon had returned with M'wanga's messenger, that monarch having specially chosen him to fill Mackay's place, on account of his being a namesake of Gordon Pasha, whose memory was revered even in countries he had never visited. Not long after, the extortion and insolence of the chiefs grew to such a pitch that Mr. Mackay found it necessary to pack up and remove the stores to Usambiro, a little further north. Hither came the bishop and Mr. Blackburn, who were soon joined by Messrs. Ashe, Walker, Hooper, and Deekes, so that there were actually seven missionaries with their bishop gathered together by the lake. A fair prospect now seemed before them. But unexpected trial was at hand.

Together with Mr. Blackburn, the bishop had made an exploring journey to Speke Gulf, and had fixed on Nasa, by the lake, as a Mission station. Returning to Usambiro, he held, in December 1887, a fortnight's conference, partly devotional, partly practical, with the missionaries there assembled. In the beginning of the following year Nasa was occupied by Mr. Hooper and Mr. Deekes.

On March 4 Mr. Blackburn was taken very ill. 'We took it by turns,' writes the bishop, 'to sit with him night and day, and gave him nourishment in small quantities at a time, and used such remedies as we all agreed upon to be most likely to benefit him. On the morning of the 12th he appeared better, but at night a sudden change came on, and he quickly fell asleep.' The bishop was much affected by his loss. Mr. Blackburn was at that time the only missionary in Unyamwezi who was familiar with the language. His wife was just then preparing to start for Africa to join him. His body was borne to the grave by his servant and boy, with six other native Christians, and his was the first burial in Usambiro. The second was quickly to follow.

On Sunday, the 25th, the little party partook of the Holy Communion together. They were expecting to separate shortly, for Mr. Walker was to start for Uganda, and the bishop was going to Nasa, to help Mr. Hooper, who was having some trouble with the chief. The bishop assisted that day in the Kiswahili services for the porters, giving them an address through an interpreter. In the night Mr. Mackay was roused by hearing him call his servant, and going to him, found that he had a sharp attack of ague. Next day he was in a high fever and delirious. Mackay, Ashe, and Walker watched him by turn, but at 9.45 that night, a fortnight after Blackburn's death, he expired. The last resting-place for the body in which he had so truly borne about 'the dying of the Lord Jesus' was made ready at once. 'It was a very rough, stormy night,' writes Mr. Walker, 'much thunder and rain, still the men worked very hard and dug the grave. Towards 4.30 the storm ceased, and in the calm we conducted the funeral. When it was just over, as we returned, the dawn was visible in a streak of crimson and gold in the east,—assuring us that though the west looked dark and as gloomy as our path, yet a bright future was in store for us as the sun rises. The bishop lies buried side by side with our friend Blackburn; they had travelled many a mile together, and now they rest together.'

Thus perished one who by the beauty of his character, by his humility of mind, his gentleness of spirit, his utter unselfishness, his calmness, and trustfulness, as well as by his singular wisdom and ability for organisation, had made himself beloved and respected by every member of the Mission of which he was called to be the head.

The telegram announcing the death of the bishop and Mr. Blackburn reached home on the day of the Church Missionary Society Annual Meeting. 'We meet,' were the opening words of the Bishop of Sodor and Man (Dr. Bardsley), at the evening meeting, 'under the shadow of a great sorrow'; and Mr. Wigram then read the telegram: 'Blackburn dead, ill ten days. Bishop Parker dead, ten days later; same sickness, ill one day.' All hearts were at once bowed with the shock of the sudden loss, and earnest were the prayers that went up to God for the mourners and for the Mission field thus bereaved. Mr. Lang in 'speaking' the Report said that the bishop was 'one in whom the Society felt they had just the right man given to them by God for a most difficult, a most delicate, and a most important work. The committee trusted him so entirely that perhaps the lesson the Lord would teach them was that they must not depend upon even the holiest and wisest agents He gives, but only and entirely upon Him.'

In the letter which arrived later on from Mr. Mackay giving the details of the sad event, he says:—

'The loss to us is indeed very great, but East Africa has lost its truest friend. We were all deeply attached to our bishop, and could not fail to admire his rare humility and deep earnestness and conscientiousness in duty. In all questions of difficulty he never acted alone, but consulted with us, and was ever ready to give up his own plan for any other reasonable one. I am sure that I state the opinion of all my brethren in the diocese when I express my conviction that it could not have been possible to find a man more admirably suited in every way as Bishop of Eastern Equatorial Africa than Bishop Parker. May our Lord guide to as successful a choice of a successor!'

One of the first acts of the bishop on reaching the south end of the lake had been to send a letter to King Mwanga, assuring him that there was no thought of taking vengeance on him for the murder of Hannington, that the Christian teachers wished to be his friends, and requesting that his subjects might have liberty to embrace whatever religion they wished. It seemed at first uncertain whether good or harm was done by this letter, though on the whole the effect was thought to be good. The king sent no written answer to it, merely a verbal message to the effect that he wished to be friendly, and inviting the bishop to send him another European. A letter written to the Baganda converts was greatly appreciated. It was read again and again, both in public and in private, and Mr. Gordon writes to the bishop concerning it:—

'Your letter to the Christians has given them much joy and consolation. I have read it on Sunday morning at worship some three or four times. In private also it has been read several times, again and again, to a few visitors who are unable to come on Sunday. . . . Henry W. Duta asked me to make him a copy of the letter, that he might read it to the Christians who frequent his neighbourhood. Yet again, Zakariya wants me to write him a copy, which he may read to the Christians who frequent his neighbourhood.'

Thus did the hearts of the converts in Uganda respond to the loving sympathy and counsel of one whom they had never seen, but whom they knew to be their friend, and thus did the bishop, after he had entered into rest, speak by his written missive to those he had died in striving to reach.

And in spite of the failure of human plans and the withering of human hopes the work of God went on.

> 'Inscrutable problems of sin and sorrow,
>   God's grand "very good" by their discords jarred;
> To-day's hopes crushed by a harsh to-morrow,
>   To *our* eyes, His plans and His workings marred.
>
> And above the floods, Love and Power conceiving
>   Their fusion into eternity's plan;
> From sin and from sorrow one Hand outweaving
>   Glory to God and goodwill to man.
>
> When our eyes shall behold Him, the Ancient of days,
>   The work will be ended; peace wrought out of strife;
> And in grand vindication of fathomless ways,
>   Out of death, resurrection—unchangeable life.'
>
> *Author of 'Copsley Annals.'*

CHAPTER XI.

THE REVOLUTION IN UGANDA.

'They said in their hearts, Let us destroy them together.'—
PSALM lxxiv. 8.

IT was a sorrowful day for the Christians when they bade farewell to the man who for nine years had been their teacher and friend, who had passed with them through trouble, and danger, and sorrow, and who had been the chief means of putting into their hands a priceless treasure, the Word of God, which they might read for themselves. To them truly Mackay might have addressed the parting words of St. Paul to the Ephesian elders, 'And now, brethren, I commend you to God, and to the word of His grace.'

It must have been about this time that the following touching letter was written by the Christians in Uganda, which was translated and forwarded to the Church Missionary Society Committee by Mr. Ashe. There appears to be some mistake in the date. Or was it begun on the date given, and finished later?

'BUGANDA MISSION, *May* 13, 1887.

'Beloved of authority in the Church of Jesus Christ, our English fathers, and all Christians who love us, our brethren. We, your Buganda brethren, write to you to thank you for the letter which you sent us. We rejoice much to hear news which came from where you are to cheer our hearts through our Lord Jesus Christ.

'We thank God that you have heard of our being persecuted. Thank God who brought our brother where you are, Mr. Ashe, and made you understand the evil which has befallen us Christians in Buganda, your children whom you have begotten in the Gospel.

'Mr. Ashe has told you how we are hunted, and burned in the fire, and beheaded, and called sorcerers, for the name of Jesus our Lord. And do you thank God, who has granted to us to suffer here at this time for the Gospel of Christ.

'We hope indeed for this thing which you hoped for us in your letter, namely, that in a short time other teachers will come to teach. And you who have authority continue earnestly to beseech Almighty God, who turned the Emperor of Rome to become a Christian, who formerly persecuted the name of Jesus as to-day this our king in Buganda persecutes us. And do you, our fathers, hope that we may not in the least degree give up the Word of Christ Jesus. We are willing, indeed, to die for the Word of Jesus; but do you pray for us that the Lord may help us. Finally, our friends, let your ears, and eyes, and hearts be open to this place, where we are at Buganda. Now we are in tribulation at being left alone. Mr. Mackay the Arabs have driven away out of Buganda. O friends, pity us in our calamity. We, your brethren, who are in Buganda, send you greetings. May God Almighty give you His blessing! May He preserve you in Europe.

'We remain, your children who love you,
'Henry Wright Duta.
'Edward,
'Isaya Mayanja.'

MWANGA, KING OF UGANDA.

The persecuted Christians were not left long alone. The boat that conveyed Mackay to the south of the lake returned in a few days with Mr. Gordon, who reached Uganda on August 18, 1887. He proceeded at once to the station of the French priests, where he got some refreshment, and received the keys of the mission house, and a couple of days later was presented to the king by the messenger who had brought him. Mwanga had by no means changed his attitude either towards the missionaries or towards their work. He wished to have a white man at his court, chiefly as a hostage, in case of any possible warlike designs upon him by the English, his mind being still uneasy about the murder of Bishop Hannington. The order prohibiting his subjects from coming to the mission house for teaching had not been cancelled. Nevertheless many, some baptized converts, and some inquirers, at once began to gather on Sundays for instruction. Most of the members of the Church Council were in hiding. For Samweli and Mika Sematimba the king watched 'as greedily as a lion watches and waits for his prey,' but the former managed to communicate with Mr. Gordon by letter. Two others, named Shem and Paulo, ventured to pay a visit to the new teacher, the latter bringing the present of an ox from the young Christian Admiral Gabunga, as his welcome. Sembera Mackay was away with his old master, the chief Isaya Mayanja, on the king's business. Henry Wright Duta and Zakariya, though under sentence of death, dared to spend some time at the mission house, hoping to escape detection. The former was useful in helping Mr. Gordon with the language, and both of them gave addresses alternately at the Sunday services, to which the people came in increasing numbers. But danger turned up, and it was found necessary for Duta and

Zakariya to return to their hiding-places, and later on there was a report that those who attended the services were to be arrested. Nothing, however, came of it.

The year 1887 passed to its end quietly. Then arrived the letters of Bishop Parker, the one to the Christians, which awakened so much interest and caused them so much joy, the other to King Mwanga. The king was at first exceedingly angry. The letter assured him that the white men did not wish to take vengeance for the murder of Bishop Hannington ; but as he would not acknowledge his guilt in the matter, he was enraged at its being taken as an understood thing. The danger to Mr. Gordon was very real, but, like David of old, he 'encouraged himself in the Lord his God.' Mwanga, however, reconsidered the letter, and said he had not at first understood it, and matters went on as before.

But it was felt that Mr. Gordon ought not to be left alone in his trying situation, and it was arranged before the death of Bishop Parker that he should be joined by the Rev. R. H. Walker. 'Bwana Orka' had an invitation by name from the king, and on Easter Monday, April 9, 1888, he started, reaching Uganda the following week. Having suffered much from fever on the journey, he waited eight days before presenting himself at Mwanga's court. Some of the converts were uneasy about this, and repeated alarming rumours they had heard. But whatever may have been the foundation for these, the good hand of God was over the missionaries, and all seemed to go well.

. Not since the arrival of Shergold Smith and Wilson, in April 1877, had such a reception been accorded to any one as now greeted Mr. Walker. The road to the palace was lined with soldiers, dressed in native style, and as the two white men passed between the ranks the drums beat, spears quivered, and a 'low tremulous cry' was kept up. Inside the royal enclosure they were met by more soldiers in white, who went through some evolutions, which formed, Mr. Gordon wrote, quite a pretty display. On entering the palace the band (drums, bugles, and horns) struck up, and the king himself with his chiefs rose up to greet them, and provided them with seats near his throne. When the court was over the soldiers in white formed in line on each side of them, and conducted them most of the way home.

The Arabs were much struck with the honour paid to the white men, and considered them high in the king's favour. His actual motive is not quite plain. It may have been a desire in this way to apologise for his former treatment of missionaries; but mingled with this there was doubtless the wish to impress Mr. Gordon and Mr. Walker by a sight of his greatness, and even, as the people themselves said, to intimidate them, so that they might not recur to any painful subject. After this the work went on quietly, not actually permitted, yet to a certain degree tolerated; and day by day the little church in Uganda grew in Scriptural knowledge, and drew others within the circle of its influence.

Mwanga had now filled the throne for nearly four years. Instead of growing stronger and more settled in his position, he was becoming more and more disliked by his subjects. Acts of violence and rapacity, unredeemed by any measures for the good of his subjects, such as had at times been undertaken by Mtesa his father, gradually alienated their loyalty. More especially had he rendered himself obnoxious to an increasingly growing and powerful party in the kingdom. These were the 'readers,' which term included both the disciples of the Protestant and Romish missionaries, and the adherents of the Mohammedans. To the 'readers' belonged many powerful chiefs, and the youth and strength of the country generally. In spite of persecution, the Christian faith still held its own at the court, and numbered among its professors some of the king's most useful officers and pages.

Mwanga had made more than one attempt to crush the new life that had risen up in his kingdom; but the more he afflicted the Christians, the more, like Israel of old, 'they grew and multiplied.' The Mohammedans had been tolerated, but even they offended the king by observing their own rites, especially with respect to food, refusing to eat of the meat slaughtered by him. At length he hatched a plot whereby he might rid himself of the principal 'readers' of both parties.

He summoned his two body-guards, both of whom were commanded by Christian leaders, the one an adherent of the Romanists, the other of the Protestants, and ordered them to follow him to the lake. He was accompanied by another guard of personal attendants, whom he had chosen from among non-readers. His plan was to send the 'readers' to execute his orders on a certain island, and leave them there to starve, while the non-readers brought away the canoes. Some rumour, however, of the king's treachery reached the 'readers,' and on arriving at the lake they refused to go farther, and returned home. It was now their turn to plot against their false master, and they took counsel together what should be done. The Christians did not wish to go to the length of dethroning Mwanga, but at length they yielded to the Mohammedans, and the matter was decided. The hour of retribution for the tyrant had come.

THE REVOLUTION IN UGANDA. 165

And yet he was not dealt with as he had dealt with others. As the two armies entered his capital by two different roads, the Mohammedans bringing with them the new king, Kiwewa, an older son of Mtesa, Mwanga collected his pages and his women, and fled unmolested to Munyonyo, on the creek. Here he obtained some canoes, and guided by a fisherman of Sesse, who had once made a voyage across the lake, he succeeded in reaching Magu, where he became a virtual prisoner in the hands of the Arabs.

Meanwhile, the revolution was effected in the most peaceful manner. The new king was enthroned absolutely without the loss of a single life. The *katikiro* fled, and took up his residence by Mtesa's tomb. Other chiefs were pardoned and deposed. The post of *katikiro* was given to a Romanist, while that of *mukwenda*, the next in importance, fell to the share of a Protestant 'reader,' Kagwa Apollo (Apollos), the same who had been so frightfully used by King Mwanga at the commencement of the persecution of 1886. Other important offices were given to Mohammedans. Liberty of worship and of teaching was proclaimed. Measures were introduced for a milder rule than had hitherto been known in Uganda, and there was general gladness and rejoicing.

Numbers of Christians now emerged from their places of concealment, and thronged around the Mission station. 'For a time,' writes Mr. Gordon, 'the Baganda came about the station like swarms of bees; from the dawn of light to the dusk of evening they crowded both sides of the house and some of the rooms.' Alphabet sheets, printed portions, Prayer Books, Epistles, Gospels, New Testaments (the latter in Kiswahili), were in great demand, and the congregation at Sunday morning service rose to the number of three hundred.

But this state of things was not to last. The new king, Kiwewa, was a mere puppet in the hands of his chiefs, and the Mohammedan party soon planned a second revolution. The Arabs and their Baganda adherents were dissatisfied at the large share of offices and dignities which had fallen to the lot of the Christians. They determined to oust them from their position, and to put an end to Christianity in Uganda. Their device was to represent the Christians as rebels, and they got up a story of an attempt being planned by the latter to place a woman on the throne, that thus Uganda might be like England in having a queen. A charge was accordingly made, and the Christians were suddenly attacked and defeated. The *katikiro* and the *mukwenda* fled, and the young Admiral Gabunga was killed. Some of the fugitives rushed to the Mission station, and Mr. Gordon and Mr. Walker were in the act of dressing the wounds of two of them, when a messenger arrived from the king, and summoned them away to a yard in the royal enclosure, where they found the French priests, and all were thrust together into a miserable hut, full of rats and vermin, where they were guarded by soldiers. The Frenchmen had been able to bring with them blankets and a scanty supply of provisions, and these they generously shared with the English missionaries. The next day some of the prisoners were marched down to their respective dwellings, to procure a present for the chief who was guarding them, and on the fifth day Mr. Gordon and Mr. Walker were taken to their station in the train of the new *katikiro*, a Mohammedan, that they might give up their goods to him. The whole place was then sacked. Mr. Walker writes:—

'At first the order was that I might keep all medicines, provisions, and sufficient bedding and clothes for the journey. You might as well have lighted a fire in the room and asked the flames to spare a few things. The *katikiro* filled my white iron box with the things he liked best, and made bundles of other things. Other chiefs did the same. All this time we heard the rabble thundering at the doors downstairs. Gordon went down with the *katikiro* to give him the keys of his store, etc. He found the whole place gutted. The doors were smashed, and some torn off their hinges, and the whole place stripped and cleared of everything. I remained upstairs and watched the most painful sight: boxes of jam and butter thrown to the crowds in the garden; men climbing in at the windows, tearing down any bit of calico they could find, emptying the contents of the medicine bottles on the floor, tearing the backs off all the books; smashing up anything they could not use.'

That night they returned to the hut, but the next day were taken to the premises of the Frenchmen, where they passed the night. The following day the whole party, including twenty natives, men, women, and children from the French Mission, were conducted down to the lake and put on board the Eleanor, where they were robbed once more of some of the few things remaining to them, Mr. Walker having even to part with his coat and trousers. They were then let go with this parting injunction:—

'Let no white man come to 'Buganda for the space of two years. We do not want to see Mackay's boat in Buganda waters for a long time to come. We do not want to see a white teacher back in Buganda until we have converted the whole of Buganda to the Mohammedan faith.'

There was a little rice and a little wheat on board

the boat. The Frenchmen had been allowed to bring away some cloth and shells wherewith to buy food. They were dependent on the Englishmen for their means of transit across the lake, while the latter depended on them for food. But a terrible disaster now occurred. They were just leaving an island where they had landed to cook some food, when a sudden blow struck the boat with such force as to make two holes in the port side. It was a hippopotamus. The Eleanor filled with water and turned over. The two English missionaries, together with the French bishop, Mgr. Livinhac, and Père Lourdel, as well as the crew of the boat, were able to swim, and quickly reached the land, which was not far off. On looking back they found, to their great joy, that the boat was still afloat on her side, and the remainder of the passengers clinging to her. By dint of shouting they roused the only inhabitant of the island, who brought his canoe to the rescue, and gradually, by threes and fours, the whole party were rescued from their perilous position. It was, however, discovered that five of the Frenchmen's boys were missing. One of the priests relates that at the moment of the accident he quickly baptized some of the boys, who though under instruction had not yet been admitted into the visible Church, and that it was these newly baptized ones, whose conduct had been such as to warrant their sudden admission, who met their death in the lake. One cannot help admiring the presence of mind and devotion of this man, however mistaken in his ideas. As for the boys themselves, we know that if with the heart they believed in the Lord Jesus Christ, as we may trust they did, it was well with them.

A large fire was made, and the wife of the owner of the canoe did her best to show hospitality to the ship-

THE REVOLUTION IN UGANDA. 169

wrecked party. The next morning their host beat his drum, to summon some of the natives from the mainland, which was not far off, to their assistance. Some boxes and sacks were got out of the boat and brought to land. Other things which were visible below the clear water were dived for by the sailors, but much was lost, and much was spoiled. The boat itself was brought safely to land, but quite unfit for use. We give Mr. Walker's graphic account of how the damage was repaired, and the journey concluded in safety.

' I went down to see the extent of the damage, and what tools, etc., could be procured. The hole was a squarish one, fifteen inches by nine, in one place, and close down by the keel; another hole was six inches by three. The tools were a caulking-iron, a spoke or hurdle shave, a hammer, and a large gimlet, and of course what nails or screws you might get out of the other parts of the boat. The fourth of the Frenchmen is a sort of cook or carpenter. He looked at the boat, and said it could be mended, but when he found there were no tools he gave up the job. I felt it a very risky business to bung up the hole, and ask thirty-three souls to trust themselves to it for a journey of two hundred miles, lasting two weeks at least. I went away into the bushes with Gordon and discussed the other alternative. He assured me that to apply to the Baganda for canoes, or to the Arabs for help, would be alike useless. I therefore undertook to patch the boat. With the spokeshave I chopped a piece of board in two. I got the board out of the bottom of the boat. One piece I fixed, with the captain's help, inside the boat over the larger hole, and fastened the ends down with wedges driven under the ribs. Then we got some rope and pulled it to pieces. Most fortunately the Frenchmen had a pail of dripping; this we worked up into the tow, and drove it in all round under our board. Then we filled up the holes with large pads of this tow and dripping from the outside, and nailed and screwed pieces of board over them. At about midday of the third day at the island the boat was pronounced to be ready for sea.

'I confess I felt bad as we rowed away from shore, miles away from land, thirty-four souls on board, and only a pad of tow and dripping to keep the water out. The good hand of the Lord was upon us. We came on slowly day by day, buying food with the Frenchmen's shells, sleeping in grass-built huts at night, or on the sandy shores by large fires. What was wetted by the rain was soon dried by the sun. After seventeen days of this life we came to the Frenchmen's house[1] at midnight. They soon knocked their surprised brethren up, and gave us a good supper and a good bed.'

The next day Mr. Gordon and Mr. Walker reached Usambiro, where they were welcomed by Mackay, and were able to enjoy a rest after all that they had undergone. But with respect to the perils they had passed through, Mr. Walker writes:—

'For ourselves, it is very pleasant to be reminded that "man does not live by bread alone"; that what we consider to be the necessaries of life are not really so; that God can easily support our lives apart from these things. We were kept in perfect health and strength without our usual food, our comfortable clothes, and snug beds. Though a good deal exposed to the heat of the sun by day, and the chill and damp by night, yet, altogether apart from any medicine, we in no way suffered. Many prayers were being offered up for us,

[1] The Mission Station at Ukumbi.

and we realised this fact by the quiet cheerfulness that was given to us in the assurance of the presence of God.'

> He is keeping watch o'er His Church below,
>   Her safety is in His hand;
> Through the night of fear, o'er the waters drear,
>   He will bring her safe to land.

S. G. S.

CHAPTER XII.

THE CHURCH IN EXILE.

'I the Lord do keep it.'—ISA. xxvii. 3.

WHEN the news reached home of the storm which burst upon Uganda in October 1888, it looked as though a full end had been made of the Mission there. The station destroyed, the missionaries driven out, many of the Christians slain, the Arabs, the foes of the work from the beginning, triumphant— this seemed the conclusion of the enterprise on which so much money, thought, pains, and prayer had been expended, and for which so many had laid down their lives. Nevertheless the friends of the Mission did not lose heart. They remembered that more than once before in the history of Missions an apparent collapse has been the prelude to better and brighter things. And they knew that 'whatsoever God doeth it shall be for ever.'[1] The work in Uganda had been HIS doing, and if for a time He had taken it utterly out of the hand of man, it was but to mature it in the shadow of His own hand.

The missionaries themselves naturally felt the apparent overthrow of all for which they had laboured, the closing up of the door through which the Gospel

[1] Eccles. iii. 14.

had reached so many. But even the one who had arrived the latest in Uganda was not discouraged. Writing from Usambiro in December, Mr. Walker says:—

'I must assure you that prayer has not been answered in the way we expected, but in a way that God saw was much better for us. Quite possibly matters were going too quickly in Buganda, and the Christians who had been made chiefs, and some of these very important ones, may have been in danger of unduly using temporal power to establish Christianity.'

But again he says: 'The work was founded upon a rock, and such a storm as has swept over the land cannot overthrow it.'

The news of the first revolution, with the fall and flight of Mwanga, reached Mr. Mackay before he had any tidings from the missionaries. Hearing that the king had escaped with a few followers, and was at Magu, on the shores of Speke Gulf, in a miserable plight, he sent to offer him a refuge at Usambiro. 'Murderer and persecutor as he had been,' writes Mackay, 'I yet have not the faintest doubt but that it becomes us to do everything in our power to return him good for evil.' The king was eager to avail himself of this friendly offer; but fearing that if he started the Arabs would follow and arrest him, he implored Mackay to come himself to his assistance. This, however, the latter could not do, as he felt that such a proceeding might affect the position of his brethren in Uganda. Later on Mwanga escaped from the Arabs, and was received by the French priests at Ukumbi.

Meanwhile, what had become of his Christian subjects, made homeless fugitives by the second revolution? In Busagala, better known as *Nkori*, or *Nkole*, to the west of Uganda, God had provided a refuge for His persecuted and hunted people. Hither, when Mwanga sought to arrest him, had fled Mika Sematimba. Hearing of the fall of his old master, Mika had set out to return home; but on the way he met his fellow-believers fleeing from the Arabs, and heard from them of what had further taken place. He at once invited them to return with him to the country where he had found an asylum, in which they were well received by the king, Ntale. Nkole is described by Mackay as the home of the royal race Wahuma, a people in many respects superior to the tribes round about them. Here most of the Christian 'readers,' baptized and unbaptized, settled for the time, while a few fled to Unyoro, and a little handful joined the missionaries at Usambiro.

From June 1889 (when letters appeared written at Usambiro the previous December), until the close of November, nothing was heard from the brethren on the shores of the Nyanza. The disturbed state of the country, owing to the resistance offered by the natives to the advance of the Germans in Usagara and Usogo, completely cut them off from the outer world, and the bearers of mails despatched by them to the coast were unable to pass. The mails, moreover, were lost, and the next letters received were of various dates, from March to September. These letters gave the history of eight months, and were full of thrilling interest. The curtain was at length lifted which had shut out the Nyanza Mission from sight, and the brethren were seen still 'holding the fort' at the south end of the lake, courageous, persevering, diligent, and hopeful, while the fact was disclosed that a large and powerful body of adherents to Christianity were holding together in the land that sheltered them, watching their oppor-

THE MISSION STATION AT USAMBIRO.

THE CHURCH IN EXILE. 177

tunity to return to their own country, and as eager as ever for instruction in the truths of the Bible.

The Protestants had chosen the chief Nikodemo (Sebwato) to preside over them, and to represent them at the court of the King of Nkole, and he was assisted by the Church Council, and by other Christian ex-chiefs. While recognising the Roman Catholics as brethren, they were often troubled by differences with them; these differences being, however, mostly political. The latter were bent on restoring Mwanga to the throne of Uganda by force of arms, after first obtaining from him the promise of religious liberty. The following letter, translated by Mr. Gordon, was written to Mr. Mackay by Sebwato Nikodemo, informing him of the condition of the exiles, and asking for advice:

'BUSAGALA, MONDAY, *March* 4, 1889.

'MY BROTHER, MR. MACKAY,—

'I, your brother, who love you much, write you this letter to salute you with much peace to-day. For many days we do not see each other, nor do I hear your news.

*   *   *   *   *   *

Now these things I tell you, my brother, that at this time the Christians are very many here at Nkole. They number about one thousand in all, with women. Then from over there in Buganda they are coming, they are coming out of their hiding-places, and on the road they do not cease to come. So for this reason we have found much trouble, and hunger in plenty; the people are nearly dying. And now all the people are wanting to return to Buganda, to fight with the people of the Koran again, a second time. Well then, we want you, our brethren, if you accept these plans, to write to us a letter quickly that we may hear. Besides, also, all matters that you have, do you write to us about, that we may understand your counsel, that you are advising and thinking about. But then, our brethren, when we left Buganda, we came in two crowds, (we) and our brothers (the followers) of the Pope. But we do not pull well together. They are always wanting to fight with us (who are) in these troubles and difficulties. However, we want you to write a letter and send it to the French priests, that they may make us come to an agreement. The end.

'I am,
'SEBWATO.'

This letter, with another from Samweli, was brought to Usambiro about Easter, by some of the Baganda, whose visit gladdened the hearts of the missionaries. Earnest advice was given them on no account to enter on a war, but to settle down quietly to cultivate the land which the King of Nkole had given them. They carried back with them to their brethren a box of books and paper—a great prize!—and also a bale of calico for the destitute amongst them, the cost of which was charged by Mr. Mackay to the Tinnevelly Fund. But at the same time that these messengers came to Mackay others appeared at Ukumbi, sent by the Romanist exiles, to invite Mwanga to return and fight for his throne. He was only too glad to accept the invitation, and having been conveyed to the mainland in the boat of Mr. Stokes, the English trader, he summoned all loyal Baganda to join him.

In the meantime a third revolution had taken place in Uganda. The Arabs were dissatisfied with their puppet, Kiwewa, and succeeded in dethroning and murdering him, not before he had killed two of the chief ministers—one of whom was Mujasi, the torturer and murderer of the first three boy-martyrs, with his own hand. There was now but one prince left, Kalema (or Karema), and he signalised his accession to the throne by putting to death all the royal family on whom he could lay his hands.

Mwanga's appeal was responded to both by Romanists and Protestants, the latter having been drawn into war before the messengers could return from Usambiro.

In the struggle three of the bitterest opponents of Christianity were slain, the former *rokino*, who had been instrumental in the death of Bishop Hannington, the murderer of Gabunga (the young Christian admiral), and the Arab Masudi, who used to translate for the king the letters that arrived from Zanzibar, and who had so often falsified them, to the prejudice of the missionaries. One cannot but call to mind the prophecy of Rev. xi. 5, concerning the enemies of the 'two witnesses': 'If any man will hurt them, he must in this manner be killed.' The old *katikiro*, also, who, though he had now and then favoured the missionaries for his own ends, had been a most bitter persecutor of the converts, was, when the third revolution broke out, burnt to death in his house.

Mwanga's attempt to regain the throne did not at first meet with success, and he was compelled to flee to the Sesse Islands, the inhabitants of which were on his side, and supplied him with canoes. Thence he advanced up Murchison Bay, and established himself on the island of Bulinguge. He then despatched messengers both to the French priests and to the missionaries at Usambiro, inviting them to send teachers for the people who were with him, and also begging their aid to recover his kingdom. The following letter was brought to Mr. Mackay by Duta, Sematimba, and Thomas Semfuma.

'BULINGUGE, *June* 25, 1889.

'To MR. MACKAY.

'I send very many compliments to you and to Mr. Gordon.

'After compliments, I, Mwanga, beg of you to help me. Do not remember bygone matters. We are now in a miserable plight, but if you, my fathers, are willing to come and help to restore me to my kingdom, you will be at liberty to do whatever you like.

'Formerly I did not know God, but now I know the religion of Jesus Christ. Consider how Kalema has killed all my brothers and sisters; he has killed my children too, and now there remain only we two princes (Kalema and himself). Mr. Mackay, do help me; I have no strength; but if you are with me I shall be strong. Sir, do not imagine that if you restore Mwanga to Buganda he will become bad again. If you find me become bad, then you may drive me from the throne; but I have given up my former ways, and I only wish now to follow your advice.

'I am your friend,

'MWANGA.'

The request put forward could not, of course, be for a moment entertained, but to the appeal for teachers Mr. Mackay was eager to respond. He had been sorely tried by the lack of reinforcements, it having been found impossible, in the disturbed state of the country, to send fresh men up to the lake. 'At Ukumbi,' he writes, 'there are sixteen Roman Catholic missionaries. Three of these mean to avail themselves of Mwanga's invitation, and are about to proceed at once to Sesse, to look after their flock. . . . Christian England, which takes such a "deep interest" in Buganda and Central Africa, has furnished the mighty force of two Protestant missionaries, Mr. Gordon and myself. How many out of our number of two are expected to be ready to respond to Mwanga's invitation, and go to supply the spiritual wants of the Protestant Christian Church in Buganda?'

Messrs. Walker and Deekes were then at Nassa, endeavouring to break up the fallow ground, and winning the confidence of the natives. But Mr. Mackay, finding that serious danger threatened them from the Arabs at Magu, sent the Eleanor to Nassa to fetch them to Usambiro. Shortly after their arrival Mr. Gordon and Mr. Walker left Usambiro in canoes sent by Mwanga, and proceeded to the island of Bulinguge, where they met with a hearty welcome from the Christians who were with Mwanga, of whom there were about one thousand, six hundred being Romanists, the remainder Protestants. The greater number of the Protestants were still on the mainland, in Budu. Here the missionaries had plenty to do in attending to the sick and wounded (some astonishing feats of surgery being performed by Mr. Walker), and several of the yet unbaptized adherents of the Mission were glad of the opportunity to receive baptism. Meanwhile the Christians on the mainland, under the command of Kagwa Apollo, marched towards Buganda, and were met by the army of Kalema. The former gained a complete victory; Kalema took to flight; and on October 11, 1889, exactly a year after the expulsion of the Christians, Mwanga was escorted back to his kingdom by those whom he had persecuted and sought to destroy out of his country. The man whom he had once cruelly wounded with his own hand, and whose valour had won him back his throne, now became *katikiro*, and all the high offices filled by the followers of the 'Book,' being about equally distributed between Protestants and Romanists.

Mr. Gordon and Mr. Walker returned with the king. They found their old dwelling-place at Natete a wilderness—mounds of earth overgrown with long grass and tall plants. But another piece of land was given them on the hill Mengo, near the capital; and the Christians immediately set to work to build a house for them and supply their ordinary needs.

But the position was still a precarious one. Kalema and his followers were not far off, prepared on the first good opportunity to make an attack on Mwanga. The army of the latter was by no means strong. 'They are not,' writes Mr. Walker, 'trained soldiers, and can only be kept up by a series of successes and constant action. Their engagements seem to take the nature of a general rush, in which every man fires his gun. If big men on the other side fall, then victory is assured to this party, and they carry all before them. I should say that the first ten minutes determine the day.' While yet on the island of Bulinguge a message had been sent by Mwanga and the Christians to the representatives of the British East Africa Company, who were at Kavirondo, to beg assistance from them; and in December letters arrived from them, together with one of the company's flags. Mwanga, in accepting the flag, virtually put himself under the company's protection; but he did not appear to understand all that such a step involved. By the time, however, that this letter arrived Mwanga was back again on the island of Bulinguge, having been driven from the mainland by Kalema's army. The missionaries were roused up in the middle of the night, and Sebwato

Nikodemo came to convey them in safety to the island, whither the king had fled. Here Christmas 1889 was spent, amid many privations, although the Christians did their best for their teachers.

But in the beginning of February 1890, a fresh supply of guns and powder having arrived in Mr. Stokes' boat, in the shape of ransom for an Arab who had been taken prisoner, Kalema was again attacked and defeated, and Mwanga with his party returned to Mengo. Here the king received Dr. Carl Peters, of the German East African Association, and signed a treaty with the Germans. This was done with the concurrence of the French priests and their followers. But the *katikiro*, with the Protestant chiefs, declined to be a party to it, considering that the king was already pledged to Mr. Jackson, of the British East Africa Company. Their refusal, however, brought about such dissension that the missionaries begged them, for peace' sake, not to hold out. The visit of the Germans seems to have had the effect of giving the people a sense of security, and they began to settle down again, to rebuild their houses, and bring their land once more under cultivation.

In spite of the desolate condition of the country from the ravages of war, and the consequent poverty of the people, one of the first acts of the Christian chiefs was to commence the erection of a church. The site chosen was on a plot of land called Kitesa (the same on which the Mission premises were situated), and the size of the building was about eighty feet by twenty-four. Some of the poles employed required six men to lift them.

But in the midst of the success and the joy in Uganda, a blow which seemed crushing fell upon the Victoria Nyanza Mission. On April 2 a man came to Mr. Walker with the message: 'Mackay is dead, and Deekes is dying.' On February 8, the man who had for twelve years been the mainstay of the Mission breathed his last at Usambiro. 'We do not want to see Mackay's boat again in these waters,' had been the words of the Mohammedans, as they drove out the missionaries in October 1888; and never again was it to touch the shores of Uganda. The vessel had done its work, and was worn out. The man who had put her together, and who had completed another boat to replace her, the man whom all Uganda knew and respected, and whom heathen and Mohammedans feared, the man whom they looked upon as inseparably connected with the cause of Christ in those regions, was never again to revisit the land for which he had toiled and prayed. But the cause of Christ, his Master and King, had triumphed over all foes and all obstacles, and before he closed his eyes on earth he was able to write:—

'The greatest, and till recently the most tyrannical power in all East Africa, is now in the hands of men who rejoice in the name of CHRISTIAN.'

'When the twilight gathers fast,
  With a quiet still and deep,
When the busy day has past,
  And the weary "falls on sleep";
When the life-long toil is o'er,
  At the setting of the sun,
Comes joy for evermore
  With the Master's word, "*Well done!*"

'Mid the tread of many feet,
  'Mid the hurry and the throng,
In the burden and the heat,
  Have the working hours seemed long?
Softly the shadow falls,
  And the pilgrim's race is run;
While through celestial halls
  Resounds the glad "*Well done!*"

Well worth the daily cross ;
  Well worth the earnest toil ;
Well worth reproach and loss,
  The fight on stranger soil !
Let us lift our hearts and pray,
  And take our journey on ;
Work while 'tis called to-day
  With the thought of that " *Well done !* " '

Author of ' *Copsley Annals.*'

CHAPTER XIII.

LABOUR AND REST BY THE LAKE.

'They rest from their labours, and their works do follow them.'—
REV. xiv. 13.

WE must turn now to see what had been going on at the south end of the lake while events so rapidly succeeded one another in Uganda.

When Mr. Gordon and Mr. Walker arrived at Usambiro, after their expulsion from Uganda, they found there Mr. Mackay and Mr. Deekes, the latter having come from Nassa on a visit. Mr. Douglas Hooper was then alone at Nassa, and he wrote on October 12, 1888: 'You will be glad to hear that our chief Kapongo still keeps quiet, and as time goes on we are getting to know the people better, and they to have more confidence in us.'

But at the beginning of 1889, feeling keenly the need of more workers, Mr. Hooper set off to return home and stir up others to go out with him. He had a somewhat perilous journey, owing to the unsettled state of the country. He was detained by the Arab chief Bushiri at the coast, after the missionaries from Usagara had been allowed to depart, on account of his having come from the interior; but at length he arrived safely in England, to make known the pressing needs of Africa.

His place at Nassa was taken by Mr. Walker and Mr. Deekes. A pleasing picture of the situation of this station is given by the former. He writes:—

'A strong wind blows all day from off the lake, and at nights the wind—which I suppose is from the land—is kept off by the hill that rises very abruptly behind the house. The cool wind, the view of the wide expanse of water with its white-crested waves, are most refreshing, and make this certainly one of the most pleasantly situated stations I have seen. Two rocks, whitewashed by the birds, I fancy, are very conspicuous, though at a great distance, as they stand out of the blue waters. Across the gulf we see the hills of the mainland. This is always a pretty sight, whether they appear to be sleeping in the distant haze during the heat of the day, or rejoicing in the ruddy beams of the setting sun. Looking east, we have a fine view, over a tree-covered plain, of a range of hills formed of broken lumps of granite, and well covered with small trees. Either by climbing the hill behind this house, or by a short walk round the base of it to the other side, we look far away over a cultivated plain of rich black soil towards Magu, a little to the west of due south. Looking more west still, we have a fine view of the open lake as far as the eye can reach, and also of the large island of Ukerewe.'

The district is well populated, and the missionaries found the people fairly friendly. But they showed no interest whatever in the Gospel message. They seemed to lead an easy and tolerably contented life, aiming no further than the supply of their immediate wants and desires. And they had not yet learned to look with confidence upon a white man, and to believe him to be their friend. 'There is no disguising the fact,' writes Mr. Walker, 'that the people want our wealth, not us.

We are allowed to live here much as their own fowls are in their villages, for the sake of the eggs they lay.'

Before six months were over the missionaries were obliged to leave Nassa. Mr. Mackay, learning that serious danger threatened them from the Arabs in the neighbourhood, sent the Eleanor, as has been already related, to fetch them away, and shortly afterwards Mr. Walker started with Mr. Gordon to join Mwanga.

Meanwhile, the station at Usambiro had not been exempt from danger. About the time of the revolution in Uganda, the chief of the place, Makolo, had been attacked by several enemies, and the Mission thus placed in considerable peril. But for timely help 'I fear,' writes Mackay, 'old Makolo's name would have to be wiped out from the maps.[1] I made,' he continues, 'every preparation to defend the Mission property and the lives of our servants, and the women and children in case of an attack, but I took strict precautions to avoid absolute hostilities, except in case of dire necessity, being prepared to pay even a heavy indemnity, should I be able to get the leaders of the invading party to consent to negotiation. Thank God, we were untouched, but we have had a weary and anxious time of watching night and day. The reinforcements which came to our aid are now returning homewards, and we are once more at peace. I ask you to join with me in devout thankfulness to our Heavenly Father for all His mercies, and His gracious protection.'

The Arabs, not satisfied with having turned the missionaries out of Uganda, did their best to get them expelled also from Usambiro. They spread about false reports of what happened at the coast, and made out that the white men were getting the worst of it in the conflict with the natives, and that even many English-

---

[1] African villages are named after their chiefs.

ALEXANDER M. MACKAY.

men had been slain, thus hoping to lower the prestige of the latter, and encourage the chiefs to attack them. From Magu they sent a message to Rwoma (the chief who had once played Hannington false) to turn them out, but he refused. They then despatched a letter to Kalema in Uganda, begging him to send a fleet of canoes and an army, to drive the white men from the shores of the lake. This request was also unsuccessful, and in spite of the bitter hostility of the Mohammedans, the Mission stations at Usambiro and Nassa remained untouched.

And all along, through uncertainty and danger, through evil report and good report, Mr. Mackay worked on unweariedly. He was revising his translation of St. John's Gospel into Luganda, and was much helped by some of the converts who had taken refuge at Usambiro. These converts also received instruction both in reading and writing, and in manual labour. One or two of them were taught to help in the printing office he had set up, whence sheets of reading matter were issued for use in Uganda, after the return of the Christians thither. He was also busily engaged in boat-building. This was a task demanding an immense amount of labour and perseverance. The forest was twenty miles distant, and the logs when cut down were too heavy either to be carried or dragged to the building place. Mackay therefore set to work and constructed a waggon, the first ever seen in these regions, and a great wonder to the natives. The month of April 1889 he spent in the forest with a gang of labourers, felling trees, and preparing and transporting the timber. 'It was very wet,' he writes, 'being the rainiest month in the year, and the long dripping grass, six feet high, was often very unpleasant. Finally, I had to give up, as the ground got too soft for the wheels.' As soon as the dry season set in the work recommenced.

A temporary boat was built under Mackay's superintendence to replace the Eleanor. But his ambition was to put together a steam-launch, to be called the James Hannington, which would greatly facilitate communication by means of the lake. He had been expecting an engineer to assist in this work, but the eagerly looked for helper never arrived, being unable to get up country. Nothing daunted by this disappointment, Mackay persevered in his work. On December 28, 1889, he writes:—

'The three-cylinder steam-engine and two steam feed-pumps stand now completely fitted and ready for the boiler. The boiler has been a more serious undertaking. . . . All these years these segments of thin quarter-inch plate have been subjected to every kind of vicissitude and rough treatment. Some parts were never apparently supplied at all, and have had to be made now. For years the unwieldy shells lay about in a cow-byre at Kagei. With great trouble they were got across the lake to Buganda. Some essential parts were more than once lost, but subsequently happily recovered. In Buganda, with its moist climate, I had the greatest difficulty to prevent the plates from being altogether destroyed by rust. There we never could get permission to erect our machinery, except at the capital, where it was useless. Subsequently I had not only the boiler shells, but also our machinery, piping, etc., shipped over here before I left the country in July of 1888. Want of proper accommodation here has also added to the damage already done to the plates, while now, after all this knocking about, I found to my amazement that what was once soft iron of 'best' quality had developed into a material of a steely, brittle nature, which cracks and splits on the first touch of the hammer. I have therefore had to resort to the process of annealing the whole—a tedious operation where no annealing furnace exists, and the best I have is a tiny, portable forge.'

Mr. Stanley at his reception at the Church Missionary House thus spoke of the work, which he had himself witnessed :—

'Mr. Mackay had a steamer building there (pointing to the map). The timber that was to form its hull was in the forest in the year 1889. The pieces of iron and steel and tubes, which were to make the engine, were scattered over all the large workroom which they had built, and I suppose the mechanics were making about three or four threads a day for one tube. Just imagine! I fancy the millennium would have come before the steamer would have been launched. There was a canoe there building, and in making into a barge, but I should have been afraid to risk my precious life in that canoe across the lake to Uganda.'

It was on August 28, the day after Messrs. Gordon and Walker had started to join King Mwanga, that Stanley arrived at Usambiro, with Emin Pasha and between seven and eight hundred people. The account of his arrival and his meeting with Mackay, with his description of the station, must be given in his own words.[1]

'Having already sent messengers ahead, that we might not take Mr. Mackay, of the Church Missionary Society, by surprise, we arrived in view of the English Mission, which was built in the middle of what appeared to be no better than a grey waste, on ground gently sloping from curious heaps of big boulders or enormous blocks thrown higgledy-piggledy to the height of

[1] *In Darkest Africa*, vol. ii., p. 386.

a respectable hill, down to a marshy flat green with its dense crop of papyrus, beyond which we saw a gleam of a line of water, produced from an inlet of the Victoria Nyanza. We were approaching the Mission by a waggon track, and presently we came to the waggon itself, a simple thing on wooden wheels, for carrying timber for building. There was not a green thing in view, except in the marsh; grass all dead, trees either shrunk, withered, or dead—at least there was not the promise of a bud anywhere, which was of course entirely due to the dry season. When we were about half a mile off, a gentleman of small stature, with a rich brown beard and brown hair, dressed in white linen and a grey Tyrolese hat, advanced to meet us.

'"And so you are Mr. Mackay? Mwanga did not get you, then this time? What experiences, you must have had with that man! But you look so well, one would say you had been to England lately."

'"Oh no; this is my twelfth year.[1] Mwanga permitted me to leave, and the Rev. Cyril Gordon took my place; but not for long, since they were all shortly after expelled from Uganda."

'Talking thus, we entered the circle of tall poles, within which the Mission station was built. There were signs of labour, and constant, unwearying patience, sweating under a hot sun. . . . There was a big, solid workshop in the yard, filled with machinery and tools; a launch's boiler was being prepared by the blacksmith, a big canoe was outside repairing; there were saw-pits and logs of hard timber; there were great stacks of palisade poles; in a corner of an outer yard was a cattle-fold and a goat-pen—fowls by the score pecked at microscopic grains; and out of the European

[1] Twelfth on the shores of the lake. Mr. Mackay had been fourteen years in Africa.

quarter there trooped out a number of little boys and big boys, looking uncommonly sleek and happy; and quiet labourers came up to bid us, with hats off, "Good-morning."

* * * * * *

'I was ushered into a room of a substantial clay structure, the walls about two feet thick, evenly plastered, and garnished with missionary pictures and placards. There were four separate ranges of shelves, filled with choice, useful books. "Allah ho Akbar," replied Hassan, his Zanzibar headman, to me, "books! Mackay has thousands of books; in the dining-room, bedroom, the church, everywhere. Books! ah, loads upon loads of them!" And while I was sipping real coffee, and eating home-made bread and butter for the first time after thirty months, I thoroughly sympathised with Mackay's love of books.'

Mr. Mackay handed over to Mr. Stanley some goods which had been lying for a considerable time at the mission house, intended for him, as well as his later mails. The earlier ones had unfortunately gone on to Uganda, and had been lost in the general pillage there. He also did his best to supply the most pressing wants of the party. He writes :—

'I could use no ceremony with them, and simply gave them plain food—"family broth"—and plenty of it. Rags, it is true, most of them were in; but I hope they left a little better provided in that way than they arrived. Only a little, mind, not much; for so great a number of Europeans at once coming on a station, when I had not much in the way of supplies, meant very little relief for each individually.'

But Mr. Stanley says that 'on the Europeans of the expedition the effects of regular diet and well-cooked food, of amiable society and perfect restfulness, was marvellous.'

The party remained at Usambiro from August 28 till September 17. Mr. Mackay writes:—

'I can assure you it was an agreeable change to me to see nearly a dozen white faces all at once, and to enjoy for nearly twenty days the pleasant company of gentlemen, mostly English.'

And Stanley thus records the impression left upon him by all that he saw:—

'Everything you saw was an evidence of industry and hard work. He (Mr. Mackay) had made his own waggons, his own fortifications, his own head-quarters; he had built the machine-house and the work-house there, and he had his people at work on the machinery. Now in the evening, before going to bed, I used to hear Mackay and his young Christians singing hymns and saying prayers. Now, it was very hard work; think of the hot sun, with the thermometer between 80° and 100, and nothing but bad water to drink. Whether filtered or cooked, it is poison all the same. Then half the morning is devoted to chaffering and bargaining with the natives. A native brings a fowl, or something else which he wants to sell, but there is nobody to buy except poor Mackay.

* * * * * * *

'He should have been head-diplomatist, or prime minister, if you please, of the Equatorial Mission, and some other body, a Bible-reader, perhaps, should have been the storekeeper and treasurer, if you like; and another party should have been set to teach the young boys day after day, instead of going far into the night after the hot day's work. These things and others we talked over ourselves every evening at dinner, from about six to half-past eight o'clock, and we could see for ourselves what the troubles of the missionaries were.'[1]

And further :—

'A clever writer lately wrote a book about a man who spent much time in Africa, which from beginning to end is a long-drawn wail. It would have cured both writer and hero of all moping to have seen the manner of Mackay's life. He has no time to fret and groan and weep. . . . To see one man of this kind, working day after day for twelve years bravely, and without a syllable of complaint or moan amid the "wildernesses," and to hear him lead his little flock to show forth God's lovingkindness in the morning, and His faithfulness every night, is worth going a long journey for the moral courage and contentment that one derives from it.'[2]

Moan, however, Mackay did make in his letters, though not for himself, but for the land and for the people whose cause lay heavy on his heart, and on behalf of whom he ceased not to put forth the most touching appeals for fresh labourers.

Stanley begged him to return home with him, but the indomitable missionary would not leave his post. 'I shall never forget,' writes Mr. Mounteney Jephson (of Stanley's expedition), 'the morning we left Usambiro. He walked part of the way with us, and wished us good-bye; and one's whole heart went out to him when he took my hand and wished me God-speed. That lonely figure standing on the brow of the hill, waving farewell to us, will ever remain vividly in my mind.' And he adds :—

'Africa is such a hard mistress to serve, and she is so pitiless to her servants.'

---

[1] From Stanley's speech at his reception at the Church Missionary House, July 1, 1890.
[2] *In Darkest Africa.*

True enough; but Alexander Mackay served a higher employer—One who never forgets or leaves unrecompensed the least thing done for Him, even to the 'cup of cold water given for His sake—One who can prosper the work of His servants, and who can call them home to rest and joy eternal, while He Himself watches over and cares for the work they have left. And but a few months longer were left for Mackay to toil under the burning African sun.

On January 2, 1890, he wrote his last message to English Christians, headed, 'Gleanings from Buganda.'[1] He says:—

'Mwanga writes, "I want a host of English teachers to come and preach the Gospel to my people." Our Church members urge me to write imploring you to strengthen our Mission, not by two or three, but by twenty. Is this golden opportunity to be neglected, or is it to be lost for ever?

'You sons of England, here is a field for your energies. Bring with you your highest education and your greatest talents; you will find scope for the exercise of them all. You men of God who have resolved to devote your lives to the cure of the souls of men, here is the proper field for you. It is not to win numbers to a Church, but to win men to the Saviour, and who will otherwise be lost, that I entreat you to leave your work at home to the many who are ready to undertake it, and to come forth yourselves to reap this field now white to the harvest. Rome is rushing in with her salvation by sacraments, and a religion of carnal ordinances. We want men who will preach Jesus and the Resurrection. "God is a Spirit," and let him who believes *that* throw up every other

---

[1] Published in the *Church Missionary Gleaner* for June of the same year.

GOD'S ACRE AT USAMBIRO.

consideration, and come forth to teach these people to worship Him in spirit and in truth.

> '" Forget also thine own people and thy father's house:
> So shall the King desire thy beauty:
> Instead of thy fathers shall be thy children,
> Whom thou shalt make PRINCES in all the earth."'

And to a personal friend who had urged his coming home to stir up fresh workers, he says :—

'But what is this you write—" Come home "? Surely now, in our terrible dearth of workers, it is not the time for any one to desert his post. Send us only our *first* twenty men, and I may be tempted to come to *help* you to find the second twenty.'

It was about a month after this that the call came to him to 'come up higher.' He had made arrangements for Mr. Deekes, his only fellow-labourer at Usambiro, who was greatly suffering in his health, to return home. But on the morning Mr. Deekes was to start, Mackay was taken with a severe attack of fever, caught probably in the draughty shed where he worked at his steamer. Being almost incapacitated himself, Mr. Deekes sent to the French priests at Ukumbi for help, but it arrived too late. Mackay was four days delirious, and on February 8, 1890, at 11 P.M., he closed his eyes on this world, and entered into rest. During those four terrible days did the needs of Africa—solicitude for the converts in Uganda, plans for the future carrying on of the work, longings for fresh labourers—press upon the brave spirit of the exhausted worker? Did disappointment, uncertainty, and yet undying hope succeed one another in that ever-active brain? We cannot tell. But He who 'giveth unto His beloved in sleep'[1] lifted him quickly out of the struggle, and bore him to rest and joy eternal. 'Now,' wrote an

---
[1] Psalm cxxvii. 2 (R.V.).

ardent friend of the cause, '*with the Lord Jesus he is at the head-quarters of the African Mission*, and rejoicing over the wonderful way in which God is making all things work together for good.'

A coffin was made for him out of wood he had cut for the boat, and at 2 P.M. on Sunday he was buried, the village boys and the Christians from Uganda singing at the grave, 'All hail the power of Jesus' Name,' in Luganda.

A burst of lament and of admiration followed his death. The world woke up to see that a humble missionary who has just passed away was a great man, and worthy of being bracketed in the roll of fame with those explorers whose names were first on its list. Stanley had already recorded his opinion of him. And Colonel Grant, the discoverer (together with Speke) of the lake on the shores of which the missionary had toiled, and where he had passed away, wrote :—

'I had the utmost confidence in him, and looked forward to the time when he would sail round the lake in his own steamer, and when we should have him amongst us to tell all he knew of that deeply interesting country which I almost love, Uganda. . . . The blow to civilisation in Central Africa which has fallen on us is not easily repaired, for a score of us would never make a Mackay.'

And Mr. Ashe, the one who knew him best in his missionary work, having lived and laboured for three years with him, writes in the preface to his book, *Two Kings of Uganda* :—

'How deep the loss of Mackay only those who knew him well and saw his work can understand. He was one of those few who look fearlessly forth and seem to see the face of the living God. He never despaired of any person or anything. Quiet he was, and strong, and patient, and resolute, and brave; one on whom you might depend. He endured fourteen years of Africa, ... fourteen years of the contradictions of men, black and white, fourteen years of dangers, fevers, sorrows, disappointments—and in all and through all he was steadfast, unmovable; a true missionary, always abounding in the work of the Lord.'

> 'Farewell! But "farewell in the Lord," brave heart,
>   Changes the word of sadness to "Rejoice":
> Though when our need is sorest you depart;
>   Though now no longer sounds your valiant voice:
> Yet not in vain your years of "daily dying,"
> Nor without fruit of joy your seed of tears and sighing,
>
> Darkness still covers deep your "darkest land,"
>   Like the scarce rent primeval forest gloom;
> But with Nyanza gleaming close at hand
>   Our hearts assemble round your victor tomb;
> And vow in God's strength, for the Crucified
> To win the land you loved so well, and loving, died.
>
> And while the man who knew and marked your worth,
>   Stanley, is welcomed with due meed of praise;
> While his just fame rings round the applauding earth,
>   Beyond the blue of these sweet April days,
> I hear your far-off welcome from the Throne,
> The Lord's approving word, the voice of heaven—Well done.'

ARCHDEACON MOULE, in *The Church Missionary Gleaner*, June 1890.

CHAPTER XIV.

A NEW ERA IN UGANDA.

'Lift up your eyes, and look on the fields; for they are white already to harvest.'—JOHN iv. 35.

EIGHT days after the lamented death of Alexander Mackay, the steamer Kaparthala reached Mombasa, bringing a party to reinforce the East African Mission. Mr. Douglas Hooper, in greatly improved health, and with a brave helpmeet at his side, the daughter of the Rev. J. Baldey, of Southsea, had the joy of bringing with him three devoted young men from Cambridge, Mr. G. L. Pilkington, Rev. G. K. Baskerville, and Mr. J. D. M. Cotter, to share his labours in Africa. They had left England on January 23, and three days earlier an interesting meeting had been held at Exeter Hall, to bid farewell to them, as well as to the party about to accompany Mr. Wilmot Brooke to the Niger. The great hall was crammed, and among those present were sixty Cambridge undergraduates who had come up together to take leave of their companions starting for the Mission Field.

The exact destination of the East African party was not fixed. 'It might,' Mr. Hooper remarked, 'be Uganda, it might be Kavirondo, it might be Ulu.' It was uncertain whether a party for Uganda would find it possible to proceed by the old route. The advance

A NEW ERA IN UGANDA.

of the British East Africa Company promised a door for labour in the vast lands stretching north-west of Frere Town, but nothing yet was known of the arrival of their agents in Uganda. The committee, in sending forth the missionaries, could not but feel that reinforcements for the lake demanded their primary attention. But the instructions were 'to proceed to Frere Town; there to wait and watch; to make all possible inquiries regarding the several routes for advance; prayerfully, in the light of these inquiries, to make such proposals to the committee as God might lead them.'

It was actually four months before the party left the coast for the interior. Following the instructions given, Mr. Hooper waited until the right course seemed to be indicated, when it was decided that the lake should be approached by the old route. But while preparations were in progress one of the party was taken seriously ill. On April 27 Mr. Cotter was seized with fever, and it quickly became apparent that he could not accompany the Nyanza expedition. In view of this disappointment Mr. Hooper telegraphed home to ask for fresh men. After a week Mr. Cotter became worse, and it was evident that he was passing away. Mr. Hooper was in constant attendance on him. A few days before his death he had his 'favourite' text, 'The blood of Jesus Christ cleanseth from all sin,' cut out of his Bible, and kept it until the end firmly grasped in his hand. On May 14 he breathed his last—the tenth who had died for East Africa.

And—so rapidly did shade and sunshine alternate in the Mission—on the same day the successor of Bishops Hannington and Parker arrived at Mombasa. The question of who should fill this post had been a subject of much thought and prayer with the committee. At length a letter from the Rev. Alfred Robert Tucker, Curate of St. Nicholas', Durham, inquiring if there was an opening for him to work as a missionary in East Africa, was followed by an invitation to him to take the leadership of the party who were to start for the Nyanza. This was at once accepted. Meanwhile the Archbishop of Canterbury, having had communication with the committee on the subject, appointed Mr. Tucker Bishop of Eastern Equatorial Africa. The new bishop was known as an accomplished artist, who had exhibited at the Royal Academy. Since his call to the ministry he had laboured devotedly among the poor. And he had obtained great reputation as an athlete, having ascended three mountains in the lake district on a single day. On St. Mark's Day, April 25, exactly fourteen years after the dismissal of Mackay, (Dr.) Smith, O'Neill, Wilson, and James Robertson, for the Nyanza, the consecration of the third Bishop of the Mission took place in Lambeth Parish Church, and the same evening he started for his distant diocese.

But while the arrival of Bishop Tucker meant a ray of sunshine for the labourers in East Africa, he himself landed in weakness and in sorrow. Several of the party on board the Ethiopian had suffered from violent sickness, caused apparently by some poisonous matter accidentally mingled with the food, and the bishop had suffered severely. The death of Mr. Cotter was the news that met him on landing. 'Cotter dead!' he writes 'Such were the tidings with which Mr. Bailey[1] greeted me when he came on board the Ethiopian on our arrival in Mombasa harbour. "Truly I had fainted unless I had believed to see the goodness of the Lord." "I was dumb, and opened not my mouth, for it was

[1] Accountant at Frere Town.

BISHOP TUCKER AND THE UGANDA MISSIONARIES.

In the back row, looking from left to right, we see Mr. F. C. Smith, Rev. E. C. Gordon, Bishop Tucker, and Rev. G. K. Baskerville; in the front row, also from left to right, we see Rev. D. A. L. Hooper, Mr. G. L. Pilkington, and Rev. R. H. Walker.

Thy doing." These words only can describe the intense anguish of my mind when with such tidings ringing in my ears, and feeling physically weak and ill, I set foot for the first time on the shores of Africa. The ladies and brethren engaged in the work at Frere Town, with the children and many natives, were gathered on the shore to greet me. In solemn silence we exchanged salutations, and then slowly the assemblage dispersed.'

That same day the funeral took place, and amid torrents of rain the precious seed, one day gloriously to unfold, was buried in the silent earth. 'The grave,' writes Mr. Bailey, 'occupies a corner of ground near the path, just shadowed by an overhanging tree.' On the coffin-lid was a text card bearing the simple words 'Jesus only.' A telegram was sent home announcing ' Cotter at rest.'

The former telegram despatched by Mr. Hooper, informing them of the illness of his fellow-labourer, and begging for immediate reinforcements, arrived in London on May 5, the first day of the Church Missionary Society Anniversary week. In it he asked that men might be sent out by the next French mail, which involved their starting the following Saturday, May 10. The telegram was read out by Mr. Wigram at the preliminary prayer meeting at Sion College, and afterwards at the service in St. Bride's Church. By 10 o'clock the next morning four offers of service had been sent in to him, and by Wednesday evening there were five more. Out of these four men were selected, Mr. J. W. Hill, of Cambridge, Messrs. J. W. Dunn and J. V. Dermott of Islington College, who had all been preparing for the ministry, and were to have been ordained on Trinity Sunday, and Mr. F. C. Smith, who had been trained for a lay evangelist. On

Saturday afternoon a hastily-got-up meeting was held at Islington College to take leave of them, and the hall was so crowded that some had to stand outside the open windows during the proceedings. The same evening the four volunteers bade farewell to home and friends, and started off for Marseilles to catch the steamer, and a telegram was despatched to Frere Town announcing their coming. 'This,' the bishop writes, 'was the second great surprise which greeted me on my arrival. Thankfulness is a cold word to express the joy and gratitude which I feel for this timely reinforcement of our missionary band.' 'But,' he adds, 'please remember that our craving for men is an insatiable one; indeed, it grows by what it feeds upon.'

But there was yet more sorrow to come. In July Bishop Tucker and his party were at Saadani, ready to start for the interior. But here Mr. Hill, who was not well when he arrived, became rapidly worse, and had to be taken to Zanzibar, where he received the utmost care and attention from Dr. Wolfendale, of the London Missionary Society. On July 20 God called him also to the home above, just one day before the party started from Saadani for the lake. They were to travel with Mr. Stokes's caravan, and had to wait some time till it was ready. Bishop Tucker remarks (the day before Mr. Hill's death): 'Although this delay has tried us very much, burning, as we are, with impatience to be off, still we can trace God's providential hand in it. Had we moved up country the day after we landed (at Saadani), we should have had Hill sick in our camp, without a doctor, and without any means of transport to Zanzibar. In the midst of trials, how helpful it is to number up one's mercies!'

The party which started on July 21, though diminished by the loss of Cotter and of Hill, was augmented by another labourer, Mr. H. J. Hunt, who resigned his office under the British East Africa Company in order to join the Mission. They reached Kisokwe, near Mpwapwa, on August 21, and after a short stay, during which thirty of the converts were confirmed, they proceeded onwards through Ugogo. Here they were exposed to considerable danger, as the natives showed some hostility towards the Germans who were travelling with Mr. Stokes, and two German soldiers were murdered. Mr. Stokes, however, managed to come to an arrangement with the chief by whose people this outrage had been committed, and the danger passed over. On September 11 the bishop wrote :—

'We are all in good health and full of hope, greatly cheered by our near approach to a country more hospitable than Ugogo. The Master has indeed been with us, keeping, strengthening, and comforting us at all times. We expect to reach Usongo about the end of September, and to be at Usambiro about October 21. But we are in the Lord's hands, and can calculate on nothing, content to live a day at a time.'

The whole party were at Usambiro at the date named by Bishop Tucker. They found that Mr. Walker had left the place only ten days before, and gone back to Uganda, whence he hoped to send canoes to take them all across the lake. The bishop would gladly have started at once, but there was no boat, that belonging to Mr. Stokes being at the sole disposal of the Germans. He accordingly set out with Mr. Hooper and Mr. Deekes for Nassa. On this journey he had his first experience of African fever, walking ten miles with his temperature at 103°. Returning to Usambiro, he was met with the sad tidings that one of the white men had died during his absence. On hastening to the Mission Station he found that Mr. Hunt had passed away, and that his remains had just been laid beside those of Bishop Parker, Blackburn, and Mackay. He says: 'I had looked forward to a career of much usefulness for him in Uganda. But God's ways are not our ways, neither are His thoughts our thoughts. And doubtless it was said of him as of David of old: " It is well that it was in thine heart." '

The six weeks during which the missionaries waited at Usambiro for the boat were altogether full of trial. At the time of Mr. Hunt's death Mr. Dunn and Mr. Baskerville were lying low with fever. Mr. Pilkington had also been attacked, but was recovering. On November 20 Mr. Dunn passed away, and the bishop wrote :—

'I am only just getting over, I trust, my third attack of fever; and I can, therefore, only add the sad, sad tidings of the death of Mr. Dunn. . . . Oh! the sad delay of the boat!'

Mr. Hooper was also stricken down, and the bishop was attacked a fourth time by fever. In spite of this, on the last Sunday at Usambiro Messrs. Hooper and Dermott were ordained priests, and Mr. Baskerville admitted to the office of deacon. When at length the boat arrived the sick ones, including the bishop, who was nearly blind from ophthalmia, had to be lifted in and laid down in the stern, and so in much weakness the Mission party, consisting of five, set sail for Uganda.

Mr. Dermott and Mr. Deekes remained behind, and after planting a hedge of euphorbia round the little 'cemetery' containing the five graves of those who laid down their lives at Usambiro, they left the sta-

A NEW ERA IN UGANDA. 213

tion in charge of a Christian Mganda, and started for Nassa.

We must now go back and see what had been passing in Uganda.

The country had suffered much from the long period of war. The ground had been left uncultivated, the Mohammedans had cut down the plantations, and devastated the land generally. Food was scarce and very dear, and the Christians often denied themselves to give some help to the missionaries. At length, in May 1890, the agents of the British East Africa Company, Messrs. Jackson, Gedge, and Martin, arrived at Mwanga's capital. They brought a treaty with them which they requested the king to sign, offering protection and support in return for the taxes of the kingdom. The Protestants were eager to accept the treaty, but Mwanga, urged on by the Roman Catholics, would not agree to it. The dissension between the two parties went so far that both threatened to retire from the country altogether. The Protestants, feeling that they could not hold their own against the attacks of the Mohammedans without foreign help, determined, in case the treaty was refused, to go with Mr. Jackson to Busoga, which had already accepted the company's protection. The Romanists, on the other hand, knew that they were not strong enough to maintain their position alone, and declared they would take their king with them, and find a home elsewhere. It was at length determined that envoys should be sent with Mr. Jackson to the coast, and that the English, French, and German consuls there should be asked to settle the matter, and that their decision should be final. By the treaty, signed at Berlin in June 1890, the spheres of German and British influence were distinctly defined, and Uganda fell to the latter.

In August another victory was gained over the Mohammedan army by Mwanga's people, assisted by the guns of the company. The rival king, Kalema, was killed, and his body brought back and buried in Uganda. Nevertheless in November, just after the return of Mr. Walker from Usambiro, there was another scare, and the king bade the missionaries prepare for a new flight. But the Christians were again victorious, and the danger passed over. The following month Captain Lugard arrived with a small force belonging to the company, and a fort was erected overlooking Mwanga's palace and capital, and the treaty was signed by the king, placing his territory under the company's protection.

Owing to the political differences between Protestants and Romanists, and the threatening attitude of the Mohammedans, the erection of the church begun in March by the Christians was somewhat delayed. But by Trinity Sunday it was completed, and was at once crowded by attentive congregations. Mr. Walker having gone to Usambiro on the death of Mackay, Mr. Gordon had his hands full. For some time school was held every morning in the church by Henry Wright Duta, for the crowds who were seeking instruction. Mr. Gordon himself was busy with the candidates for baptism, with translational work, with the sick, and with all the thousand-and-one things that fall to the lot of a solitary missionary in charge of a station. A 'committee for translation' was formed from among the Christians, all being 'men who had suffered reproach for the cause of Christ.' The Gospel of St. John, begun by Mackay, was completed, and St. Mark was taken in hand.

A fortnight after the advent of Captain Lugard, on December 27, 1890, the third Bishop of Eastern

Equatorial Africa—the first to reach this distant goal —landed in Uganda. The voyage across the lake, which occupied twenty-three days, had been a tedious and in some respects a perilous one. On one occasion, a storm having suddenly risen, the wind caught the mainsail, which the crew had tied to the side of the boat, and before they had time to obey the order of Mr. Hooper and loose it, the boat heeled over, and in a moment more all must have perished. But in the good providence of Him who watched over them the sail gave way to the strain and split, and the boat righted herself. The cool lake breezes brought new life to the sick and weak, and with fresh hope and courage they set foot on the land so long looked forward to. As they camped on the shore from time to time on their way up Murchison Creek crowds gathered about them, begging for books and for instruction; and Mr. Pilkington, who had picked up some of the language, was surrounded by eager listeners. At length they reached Mengo, and on Sunday, December 28, Bishop Tucker stood to speak (through an interpreter) to fully a thousand Christians in the church they had themselves built. 'It was a wonderful sight!' he writes. 'There, close beside me, was the *katikiro*—the second man in the kingdom. There, on every hand, were chiefs of various degrees, all Christian men, and all in their demeanour devout and earnest to a degree. The responses, in their heartiness, were beyond anything I have heard, even in Africa.'[1]

The following day the new-comers were received by the king. They were welcomed with blowing of trumpets and beating of drums, and their seats were placed at the king's right hand. A more interesting

---

[1] At Frere Town, and at Kisokwe, Mpwapwa, where the bishop had been much impressed with the heartiness of the worshippers.

interview was that held with the native Church Council, at which the bishop announced a confirmation to be held shortly, and gave the members earnest advice respecting their own spiritual life.

The bishop was most anxious that the Church in Uganda should be organised upon a sure basis, and the foundation laid for a future native ministry. Six young men were chosen to be set apart as lay evangelists. Three of these, Henry Wright Duta, Sembera Mackay, and Mika Sematimba, had already refused chieftainships from the king because they desired to devote themselves to the work of teaching. The other three were Paulo Bakunga, who had been the keeper of Mtesa's tomb, Zacharia Kizito, leader of the deputation which had waited on Stanley when he arrived in Nkole during the residence there of the exiled Christians, and Yohana Mwira, baptised in 1883 by Mr. O'Flaherty. Their maintenance was to be undertaken by the Church members.

On January 18 the first ordination was held in Uganda, when Mr. Gordon and Mr. Baskerville were ordained priests. It was followed by the confirmation of seventy converts, men and women. 'Many of them' writes Bishop Tucker, 'had suffered persecution for the name of Christ. Many had been deprived of their earthly all. All were deeply in earnest, and those who prepared them and presented them were greatly struck by their deep sincerity and heart devotion to the cause of Christ. The lay evangelists were set apart on the 18th; and this service was followed by the administration of the Lord's Supper to the newly confirmed. The quiet solemnity of this service,' writes the bishop, 'I shall never forget; the future of the Buganda Church seems, humanly speaking, to be wrapped up in these earnest, devoted men and women, who with quiet reverence and gentle footsteps came forward to receive of their ministers the elements of Christ's body broken and His blood shed.'

The stock of Swahili Testaments brought by Bishop Tucker was soon exhausted. Men willingly brought a sum equal to three months' work in payment for one of these precious books. A princess, sister of the late King Mtesa, came one day to see the bishop. She was by nature, he tells us, a taciturn woman, and she sat half an hour in silence. At last she summoned up courage to ask if she could have a Testament. On receiving the volume her whole demeanour changed. She smiled, laughed, clapped her hands. 'I almost thought,' says the bishop, 'she would sing; but at any rate she told me that her spirit was singing within her for joy.'

One of the matters that claimed the bishop's care during the short four weeks spent in Uganda, was the misunderstanding between Protestants and Romanists, which had reached a point threatening considerable danger. He invited Père Brard, the then head of the Romanists' station (Père Lourdel having lately died), to a conference, and the grievances of either party having been written, they were carefully discussed, and the event was an amicable settlement, at least for the time, certain matters relating to property, which could not at once be disposed of, being left to the adjudication of the company.

The Christians provided Bishop Tucker with the necessary supplies during his sojourn amongst them, and would have been only too glad to keep him longer. But he and his brethren felt that the right course was for him to proceed home to England at once, to relate what he had seen, and bring out fresh labourers to occupy the fields for work opening on all sides. Accordingly, on January 22, 1891, he and Mr. Hooper bade farewell to the missionary band, and to the warm-hearted converts, many of whom accompanied him some way along the road to the lake. Their last morning on the shores of Uganda must be described in the bishop's own words.[1]

'We were astir before sunrise. The purple flush of the dawn was brightening when there came, on the stillness of the morning air, a sound which stirred our souls to the very depth. What was it? From some little distance, from a native hut which we could see but dimly in the half-light, there came a voice from one pleading with God in prayer; then came the response; then once more all was still. What was the meaning of it? These were the voices of Christian men and women engaged before sunrise in family worship. They were men and women who only a few years ago were living in all the darkness of heathendom. Could we, as we stood there on the Uganda shore for the last time, could we have had a more touching proof of God's work of grace in the hearts of the people, and of the power of the everlasting Gospel to change men's minds, turning them from darkness to light, from the power of sin and Satan unto God?'

Bishop Tucker reached England on May 23, but before his arrival some of the reinforcements he had come to ask for had already started for Africa. Mr. Ashe had set out for his former field of labour, with a party of five others. One of these had, like Cotter and Hill, to lay down his sword at the very outset. The Rev. G. H. V. Greaves died at Zanzibar just a month after reaching Africa. He had been most carefully nursed at the Universities' Mission, and was

[1] In his speech at Exeter Hall on June 2, 1891.

buried in their cemetery, close to Livingstone's old servant Susi. The words of John iii. 16 were, at his own request, inscribed on the tomb of the *fourteenth* who had died for East Africa.

Meanwhile the Church in Uganda was not slow in setting to work. Mr. F. C. Smith proceeded to Busoga, to the village of the chief Wakoli. Two of the native Christians commenced teaching in the village of Lubwa, the chief who had murdered Bishop Hannington, and a third started work in another place. Mr. Walker went to Budu, a province south-east of Uganda, which is in charge of one of the king's great officers, the *pokino*, who is none other than the old Christian chief Nikodemo Sebwato. With Mr. Walker were Mika Sematimba and Yohana Mwira, and all three were supported by the *pokino*, Mr. Walker himself living entirely on native provisions. A little church has been built, and there is a good attendance at the services. Native evangelists have also begun work in Usukuma.

Much has been hoped for from the construction of a railway from Mombasa to the lake, which was commenced by the British East Africa Company in August 1890. The project has, however, not yet been carried out, owing to the enormous expense of the work, if undertaken without the support of Government. But the cost of maintaining their position in Uganda without an easier means of transit from the coast was found by the company to be so serious, that after much consideration they reluctantly sent orders to their agents there to withdraw. It was felt by the friends not only of the Mission, but of Africa generally, that this would prove a fatal blow to the hopes entertained for the country. The agents of the company were looked upon in Uganda as the representatives of England, and their abandonment of the land they had pledged themselves to protect would produce an utter loss of confidence in the power and good faith of the nation. The prestige of England in the Dark Continent would suffer severely, even if it were not hopelessly lost. Of the danger to the missionaries and their converts in Uganda, who are now unavoidably connected in the native mind with the agents of the company, Bishop Tucker spoke most touchingly in his farewell address at the Anniversary Meeting of the Gleaners' Union on October 30. A totally unexpected scene followed. As the bishop sat down, Mr. Eugene Stock rose to speak. He told the meeting (we quote from the report in the *Church Missionary Intelligencer* for December) 'that the order (for the withdrawal of the Company's agents) had gone out, and was probably not far from Uganda at that moment. The company had so far "taken their dividends out in philanthropy." They could only countermand the order if £40,000, the estimated cost of maintaining their representative in Uganda for another year, could be guaranteed in the course of about a week. Individual members of the company and their friends could pledge themselves to some £20,000, if the Church Missionary Society could raise £15,000. But the Church Missionary Society, as a society, could not raise money for such a purpose, though its members in their private capacity might do so.' An appeal had just been put forth in the names of Bishop Tucker, Sir John Kennaway (President of the Society), and General George Hutchinson (a former Lay Secretary), and this was commended to the meeting. The collection of course could not be utilised for the purpose, but it was suggested that slips of paper, naming amounts that might be promised, could be put into the boxes as they passed round. The question seemed to be at that moment trembling in the balance : 'Shall Uganda be saved?' and fervent prayer went up that the answer from on high might be manifestly given, and might go forth from that meeting. Yes ! And so it was ! Into those boxes went slips of paper promising various amounts, larger or smaller. £5,000, £500, £50, were promised that night, together with lesser sums, and a gold watch and a bag of rupees were sent up to the platform, while one paper bore the words : 'My four freehold plots of ground shall be given for Christ.'

In a few days more other sums followed, and quickly the telegram was despatched to cancel the order for withdrawal, and save, not only Uganda, but the fair fame of England, among the Africans.

Not that the work is done. There is the railway yet to be constructed, and the construction of a railway is, as was remarked in the *Times* of September 28, 1891, 'the keystone of the whole fabric of East African enterprise,' and would be the surest means of putting an end to the slave trade which desolates those lands that ought to be won for Christ. But a preliminary step has been taken in the sending out of Captain J. R. S. Macdonald, R.E., in charge of an expedition for making the necessary preliminary survey.

Another important matter affecting the welfare of Uganda and of the Mission is the placing of a steamer on the lake. It is well known that this has long been under consideration, and that a sum of money was raised by friends for the purpose. The Committee of the Church Missionary Society have decided not to accept even the gift of a steamer, as they do not feel justified in undertaking the responsibility of the annual outlay required to keep it up. This, therefore, is left to the company to provide. Meanwhile, we are told that a German expedition has left Berlin with the intention of laying out a dockyard and launching a steamer on the Nyanza.

More directly connected with missionary work is the sending out of copies of the Word of God to the people who are thirsting for them. Swahili Bibles, and copies of those books already translated into Luganda, are eagerly sought after. And herein lies the antidote to the teaching of the Romanist priests, who, together with their converts, greatly outnumber the Protestant missionaries.

The political differences between Protestants and Romanists are very serious. The Protestants, having helped to restore Mwanga to his throne, object, not unnaturally, to the power being little by little monopolised by the Romanists, instead of being divided, as at first agreed, between the two parties. Such of them as have made a mere nominal profession of Christianity are tempted to go over to the side of the majority, and some have actually done so; and the situation generally is fraught with much danger and uncertainty.

What is in store for Uganda in the future we cannot tell. The situation of the country and the many admirable qualities of the people seem to make it a fitting centre whence the light of the Gospel may go forth to the nations around. Clouds indeed loom darkly on the horizon. But the story of the sixteen years since the Victoria Nyanza Mission was first proposed in 1876, is a wonderful example of the way in which, with or without human instruments, God carries on His own work, makes the 'wrath of man' to praise Him, brings victory and gladness out of seeming defeat and disappointment, and turns 'the shadow of death into the morning'!

> Oh, let the message fly faster!
> The time is speeding away,
> And the thrilling voice of the Master
> Speaks, 'Work while 'tis called to-day.'
> Then send forth the news of gladness,
> Let its echoes ring far and wide,
> And joy shall banish all sadness
> At the coming of harvest-tide!   *S. G. S.*

www.ingramcontent.com/pod-product-compliance
Lightning Source LLC
Chambersburg PA
CBHW031818230426
43669CB00009B/1185